A BRIEF HISTORY OF

OVER SHARING

A BRIEF HISTORY OF

OVER SHARING

ONE GINGER'S ANTHOLOGY OF HUMILIATION

SHAWN HITCHINS

Published by ECW Press
665 Gerrard Street East
Toronto, Ontario, Canada M4M 1Y2
416-694-3348 | info@ecwpress.com

To the best of his abilities, the author has related
experiences, places, people, and organizations from his
memories of them. In order to protect the privacy of
others, he has, in some instances, changed the names of
certain people and details of events and places.

LIBRARY AND ARCHIVES CANADA
CATALOGUING IN PUBLICATION

Hitchins, Shawn, author
A brief history of oversharing :
one ginger's anthology of humiliation
/ Shawn Hitchins.

ISSUED IN PRINT AND ELECTRONIC FORMATS.
isbn 978-1-77041-326-9 (softcover)
also issued as: 978-1-77305-058-4 (PDF)
978-1-77305-059-1 (ePUB)

1. Hitchins, Shawn. 2. Comedians—Canada—
Biography. 3. Entertainers—Canada—Biography.
I. Title.

PN2308.H59A3 2017   792.702'8092
C2017-902399-3   C2017-902978-9

Editor for the press: Crissy Calhoun
Cover photos: Jen Squires
(jensquiresphotographer.com)
Cover typography: Christopher Rouleau
(christopherrouleau.com)

The publication of *A Brief History of Oversharing* has been generously supported by the Canada Council for the
Arts, which last year invested $153 million to bring the arts to Canadians throughout the country, and by the
Government of Canada through the Canada Book Fund. *Nous remercions le Conseil des arts du Canada de son
soutien. L'an dernier, le Conseil a investi 153 millions de dollars pour mettre de l'art dans la vie des Canadiennes et des
Canadiens de tout le pays. Ce livre est financé en partie par le gouvernement du Canada.* We also acknowledge the
support of the Ontario Arts Council (OAC), an agency of the Government of Ontario, which last year funded
1,737 individual artists and 1,095 organizations in 223 communities across Ontario for a total of $52.1 million,
and the contribution of the Government of Ontario through the Ontario Book Publishing Tax Credit and the
Ontario Media Development Corporation.

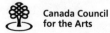

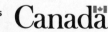

PRINTED AND BOUND IN CANADA

PRINTING: MARQUIS   5   4   3   2   1

To Harrison Ford
⇀ for making me gay ⇀

To my Father

~ for making me a comedian ~

SET LIST

"At least I know who I WAS when I got up this morning, but I think I must have been changed several times since then."

Alice's Adventures in Wonderland

WILL THERE BE SHADE?

Every six months, I stand in front of my dermatologist, wearing my best and cleanest pair of underwear.

Sockless and acting nonchalant, I wait for the examination to begin, anticipating a worst-case diagnosis. My dermatologist, Dr. Levi, begins by sliding a manila envelope out from my patient chart. The kind of envelope that is written into thrillers where a politician is blackmailed with a series of adulterous snaps. *Black-and-white photos captured through a vertical blind reveal a middle-aged congressman kissing a sex worker. His shameful secret hidden safely . . . for a price.*

Scandalous contents like that would be a welcome reveal.

Unfortunately, my envelope contains medical photos: shot in a medical photography studio, by a medical photographer (a technician) who climbed his way out of Service Ontario and who is biding his time (making living people appear dead) until a position in the coroner's office opens. The photos are securely stored in my doctor's office and I would be mortified if they were ever leaked, not because they are NSFW but because they are so asexual it would create an entire new genre of pornography called pity porn.

In the photos, a younger (twinkier) me stands in Calvin Klein underwear recreating awkward contrapposto positions found only on the tombs of pharaohs. The runway stances highlight the natural beauty marks that decorate my body. I am a hundred Cindy Crawford moles in one mortal. In the more risqué shots, I pull down my underwear to reveal my buttocks while internally trying to feel *Costco Connection* sexy for the camera. The entire lousy shoot cost me forty-five dollars and to this day these glossies remain the only nude photos of me (with my head not cropped off).

I should have demanded the negatives.

The photos are an archive, a mapping of the layers of cells and groupings of melanin that compose my skin, used to compare *then* to *now* (and future nows), a control to measure change.

"You're a comedian? That's a terrible job!" Dr. Levi remarked during one of my first visits as he scanned the giraffe-like patterns on my shoulders.

I admit: it is a terrible fucking job.

But then I reminded my doctor that he actually went to medical school to stare at moles, herpes, and plantar warts until retirement, and that half his patients are white males above the age of sixty-five. (The same demographic of towel-less men who abuse the complimentary hand dryers in gym locker rooms, drying their saggy ass cracks and fanning their foreskins for everyone to see.)

Most of my appointments with Dr. Levi consist of playing this terrible pointing game called *Cancer? Not Cancer*. The rules are simple: I point to the various parts of my body then ask, "Cancer?" and Dr. Levi shakes his head and says, "Not cancer." We go back and forth like this until Dr. Levi points to something I didn't see and says, "Cancer!" And we laugh.

Levi plays this game for a living, which is probably why he wants to outsource his routine to someone less qualified, like a loved one. Dr. Levi once prescribed me a long-term relationship so that I could have someone "I trust" to "perform weekly mole checks" on my back. Because according to the medical community, the most successful relationships occur when all walls of intimacy are shattered, all mystery is eviscerated, and all Friday nights are spent watching reruns of *Gilmore Girls* while checking each other's moles for irregular borders. Only within the context of a stable relationship can one take a selfie of a heart-shaped precancerous lesion and text it with a personalized, "Does this look funny, bae?"

Dr. Levi checks everywhere: the soles of my feet, my armpits, even my "down there" area. He is an eccentric professional who refuses to say the words "penis" or "vagina" because they "creep him out." Instead, he uses euphemisms during his examinations. Once, Levi took the Bic pen he was writing with and used it to examine *down there*. First, he shimmied the blunt end of the pen under my left testicle and lifted it up-and-out, forming a waterfall of scrotum. He inspected the skin underneath. *Left side all good.* Then he swooped over the right side and sawed his way back and forth until he got another gander. *Right side all good.* Finally, he lifted the pen up towards his mouth, placed the end that had been wedged under my balls to his lips, clamped down on the plastic tube, and hummed a pensive yet satisfying *hmmm*.

I just stared at his mouth sucking on the pen.

I teabagged my doctor by proxy.

Levi's bedside manner is more appropriate for a bunk bed in a hostel, and it's a rare occasion that I don't leave his office biopsied into a piece of Swiss cheese, but if you're going to hear you have a dysplastic mole over the phone, it's best delivered like this:

"Hey Shawn! Don't panic! You're not going to die, but let's just say . . . you owe me a bottle of wine."

—

The largest organ on my body is a ticking time bomb. At some point, I will confront melanoma, more melanoma than the scars on my body already chronicle. This is the joy of being a redhead (a Ginger, a Ranga, a Stop Sign, a Viking Sunset); this is the fate of having Fitzpatrick Type 1 skin (a medical classification meaning you always burn and never tan). And I struggle with my inability to remedy this situation simply because I cannot undo the damage from the past.

I can't negotiate with my childhood sunburns, the early exposure that now causes things shaped like the United Kingdom to appear on my upper thigh. As an '80s baby, I had the full force of the sun blazing on me before Bill Clinton single-handedly fixed the ozone layer. Back then, baby oil was applied liberally to a child's skin before they danced naked in a playpen filled with quicksand, ticks, and rusty nails while fighting off rabid dogs and stranger danger with a bat made of lead paint and asbestos. I have blistered and peeled more layers of skin than a California corn snake: these are irreversible circumstances.

As a grown adult, you would hope that your skin would engage an innate survival tactic by producing a gorgeous even tan. *Let's call it "the Italian Instinct."* I had a roommate who had this theory that if I went to a tanning bed, I could build up a tolerance, so she bought me a package of ten sessions at a posh Yorkville tanning salon as a Christmas gift. I went to one session. I stripped down, lubed up my body with this gel, then slid into a non-stick neon coffin. I just lay there, illuminated in blue light, my skin searing, while the Backstreet Boys were piped in through a speaker. Our experiment didn't work and now every time I hear "Quit Playing Games (With My Heart)" I stop, drop, and roll.

I cannot will my body to generate a defense mechanism. I can't generate a fluffier tail for winter like a squirrel. I can't sweat blood to protect myself from the sun like a hippopotamus. So now I live my life like an indoor cat.

I don't tan.

I don't go to the beach.

I know what time of day I can walk outside and in what direction, depending on the placement of the sun for the given calendar date.

I wait at traffic lights in the shadows cast from a building instead of at the curb.

I have a Lycra UV-blocking swimsuit that makes me look like a blue superhero sausage.

I wear unflattering wide-brimmed straw hats.

Whenever a friend invites me to an "awesome summer barbecue," I immediately ask, "Will there be shade?" Then I demand the architectural blueprints of their home and a three-hundred-and-sixty-degree panoramic shot of the backyard as POS (Proof Of Shade) before accepting their invitation. I calculate the day's UV Index cross-multiplied by the time of sunset to determine what grade of SPF I should apply (the answer is never less than aluminum foil). Then I consult a local arborist and commission an environmental assessment to detail the species of shade trees indigenous to the postal code I'm traveling to. Finally, I soak myself in a vat of toxic sunscreen and allow it to seep into my lymph nodes. Then and only then will I enter an "awesome summer barbecue" two hours late and dressed like a slutty gay scarecrow.

This is the reality of being me.

I was born high-maintenance.

DENIAL IN EGYPT

I am from Egypt, Ontario.

I will not embellish this statement by harkening back to my ancestry. I will not glorify it by saying, "I'm from Egypt, Ontario, but . . . my grandparents and great-grandparents were World War I– and Depression-era immigrants from England and Denmark." I do not suffer the Canadian fear that by admitting you are from South-Central Ontario (and only from South-Central Ontario), you declare your origins to be incredibly ordinary — which mine are.

I am from Egypt, Ontario.

My heritage is an intersection.

Two country roads carved a path through rolling hayfields, lush pastures, and low swampland, and at their crossing families gathered. The surrounding cattle and sod farms caught in its radius created a border that was upheld and defended by proud farmers who agree, "It's always a great day in Egypt!"

My family lived in a small discharge-yellow home situated on the northeast corner of Egypt's main (and only) junction. Adjacent to my family home, in opposite corners, sat the Egypt Hall and the Egypt Church of the Nazarene — simply named for exactly what they are, no-frill structures for mayonnaise-based celebrations. Either one of these landmarks could have been adorned with the honorable name of humorist Stephen Leacock, whose childhood home lay unmarked by historical plaque only several fields away. However, Leacock is neither Egyptian nor immortalized as such, and if you've read Leacock, you are most definitely not from Egypt.

The southwest corner remained an open field lined with crab apple and pear trees that bore inedible fruit. The land served as an important catch basin for speeding cottagers who would find their cars suddenly airborne and upside down after underestimating Egypt's infamous death jog in the road. For decades, my family has pried Torontonians from their engulfed vehicles, dragged them to safety, ushered them into ambulances, whispered a little prayer, and declared in police statements: "Someone should really put up a sign about that corner."

There is still no sign.

Egypt is not a town (you must drive fifteen minutes to get to town) but a mindset. It's an amalgamation of family clans where it's easier to flat-out accept everyone as a cousin than it is to map bloodlines and calculate generations of separate family trees grafted together and struck by lightning. This is my poetic understanding of what it means to be conditioned like an inbred without actually being genetically inbred: you're either a cousin or you're an outsider.

My mother, Linda, and my father, Ian ("a townie"), partitioned an acre of land off my grandfather's farm in 1975, and they built their home from architectural plans selected out of a catalog of prefabricated bungalow dreams. This succession plan was established by my grandfather Clarence Smockum, who bought side-by-side farms with his brother Kenneth in 1952, and alongside their respective wives, Elsie and Norma, they tilled the earth, raising crops, herds of cattle, and flocks of children. Although we carried the last name Hitchins, we were very much raised as Smockums.

Clarence was the very definition of an Ontario farmer, only he had magical powers. He could witch for water using a forked branch; herd the cattle from the pasture to the feed trough every morning by calling "ko-bah"; shoot a raccoon out of a tree without looking; mend tools, tractor parts, and fences using only baler twine; drive his brown GMC as slowly as his red Massey Ferguson (and his tractor as fast as his truck). He owned a hunting dog named Amos who was immortal and could change breeds every two years.

Clarence struggled after Elsie died of pancreatic cancer in 1981. He would live in his farmhouse for a handful of years as an unhappy bachelor, which countered his nature as a vibrant, stout man with flat feet and a wreath of gray hair. When he met Helen Westgarth, a widow from nearby Udora, she arrived in Egypt with her own set of powers. Helen could switch stoplights to green by snapping her fingers, transform balls of yarn into beautiful blankets, sear a roast so intensely the smell wafted over hayfields and signaled Sunday-night dinner, paint an animal on any piece of wood. Helen also brought with her a large family with even more cousins, and Egypt grew tenfold on her arrival. Although Clarence and Helen would never marry, they became companions until his death in 1996, at the age of sixty-nine. Helen became the only grandmother I would know.

My other grandfather, Albert Hitchins, was a solitary man who lived in town, in nearby Sutton. After his wife, Ethel, died in 1983, he remained a widower until his death in 2006, at the age of ninety-four. His only companion during that time was Chester, a foul-breathed, flea-ridden, ginger-haired dog with skin tags. Albert lived a short drive away, but we hardly saw him, except on the occasional Friday night when my parents would go curling and needed a babysitter. Then Lori, my older sister, and I would sit on Albert's twill couch eating meatball subs and drinking A&W root beer while watching WWF wrestling and John Wayne westerns until late the next morning: that is, experiencing the life of a townie.

Albert was a reserved man who carried the coldness of someone born in England at the threshold of World War I. He didn't own a car or a set of dentures. He walked wherever he went and he ate the same thing almost every day: hamburger goulash with a side of HP Sauce. He was poor but resourceful, and he was ribbed for refilling old glass Coca-Cola bottles with water and storing them in his fridge. *We could have been scions of bottled water.* His home was small, dark, musty-smelling, and it seemed mathematically impossible that a family of seven could have been raised in such tight quarters. Inside his home it seemed as if time had stopped in 1983 when Ethel died, but his property was vibrant and full of life.

There was a lush garden of mature trees, manicured hedges, and long thoroughfares of grass separating wide beds of perennial flowers and allotments of vegetable plants. Every July, the entire Hitchins family gathered in Albert's garden for a barbecue, an event that inevitably ended in either an anxious spat between siblings or a playful water fight that turned into an anxious spat between siblings. It was an opportunity to reacquaint ourselves with the other cousins (the near strangers) who lived in subdivisions, in cities, and out of province. Lori and I were recognized as the redneck cousins (the near strangers) who lived in the middle of a hayfield and didn't have access to cable or MTV.

My mother has spent her life on the same acreage, and the stories of her childhood sound straight out of pioneer times. She attended a one-room schoolhouse where a strap was used for enforcement, slates and chalk were writing implements, and a commode (an indoor open well of sewage capped with his-and-hers toilet seats) was the only option. (Indoor plumbing, even in homes, was an unaffordable luxury until the late '60s for most country dwellers.) The children of Egypt were eventually bussed to a regional public school built on a swamp, and the schoolhouse was repurposed as a hall for the Egypt Women's Institute, before changing hands several times and then, in 1989, being razed.

On that day, our front lawn was lined with fellow Egyptians who watched the decrepit building crack open with the force of four tractors pulling in opposition. The adults mourned the brittle snapping of the walls with tears, while the children obnoxiously cheered the revving of tractors and the giant plume of dust. The community banded together and built a new hall. The men worked in their spare time, after work and on weekends, year-round to construct the new building. The women made meals and supervised the children as they collected roofing nails and scrap from the ground and chipped mortar off the old red bricks so they could be resold.

When the building was complete, the preserved schoolhouse bell was placed on its steeple as a symbol of pride. Its ringing signaled an Egyptian Spring filled with corn roasts, hay-wagon rides, community dances, and baseball games. Brown mesh trucker hats branded with "Beautiful Downtown Egypt" seemed to be the latest fashion craze. Egypt got its own Little League team, the Egypt Camels, and we practiced on a baseball diamond cut into a corn-field. It was our very own Field of Dreams. When lightning struck the school bell in 2012, the hall burned to the ground. The very next day, the community banded together (once again) and began rebuilding the structure exactly as it was. Yet they bemoan that the brand-new community hall "doesn't feel the same." Change is not a welcome force in Egypt, never has been and never will be.

During the much-loathed Ontario NDP government of the early '90s, the prime farmlands of Egypt were slated to become Toronto's "megadump." Protest signs decorated the lawns and fences, simply stating, "NO DUMP!" This political action was my very first venture into scrapbooking as I clipped various articles from the *Georgina Advocate* and the *Era Banner* and proudly pasted them into a book I evocatively titled "The Dump." At the height of the anger, the surrounding hamlets banded together and a convoy of hundreds of tractors, trucks, and cars drove at a farmer's pace down the 404 highway and circled the grounds of Queen's Park, halting busy city life. In a burgundy Astro van inching down the Don Valley Parkway, I got my first glimpse of Toronto's sky-line, including the CN Tower . . . This was "The Big Smoke" that threatened our very existence. Egypt was spared Toronto's refuse, the city repressed its garbage crisis down an abandoned mine shaft somewhere else, and our sanctity continued.

While it's not my intention to give a full and detailed account of the slack-jawed terrarium in which I was raised, it is important for me to establish that, like a veal calf, I was nurtured and raised for a specific fate. Like many young gay men from small towns who came into their sexualities in the shadow of the AIDS crisis and before *Ellen* and *Will & Grace*, when my Rockwellian existence soured I became an outsider, no longer part of some greater whole that can only be explained in farm-speak. There is a copacetic relationship between the farm animals and the barn that houses them. The shelter provides a safe refuge for them, and the heat and moisture created by the livestock maintains the structural integrity of the foundation. The hayloft above stores food for the animals while insulating the interior wood from harsh winters. When you remove the animals and their food from the barn, the foundation dries out, the wood rots, and the structure falls to ruin. My exodus from Egypt triggered neither plagues of frogs nor water-into-blood transformations, but I no longer contributed to the provincial mindset that reinforced Egypt's existence and Egypt could no longer provide me shelter.

I was raised with an intense sense of belonging and a blind sense of comfort that I've desperately tried to regain since I lost it. But normalcy has evaded me at every turn. So I surrendered to the margins and learned to survive in the undefined. I have done many bizarre things to push myself or to test my breaking points, to release tension the way an athlete stretches a cramped muscle. I have fallen apart more times than what I will admit to, not because I am fragile or weak, but because this is the reality of the stateless. We push to create a space for ourselves, and often to our detriment we are both the barn and the cattle. And sometimes we burn it and everything down like a nineteenth-century lunatic.

I moved to Toronto and quickly learned that living in the Big

Smoke is just like living in a small town. Both are full of gossips, bigots, boozers, sluts, addicts, criminals, and Jesus freaks, except living in a city I'm not related to any of them.

Only with the self-flagellation of an elastic band did I erase the distinct twang (a confusing hybrid of American Midwest and Canadian East Coast) that is unique to my family. Every harsh snap of an elastic band against my wrist may have removed a "t" from the word "across" or replaced "eh" with a period, but no amount of office-supply therapy could unknot a crocheted way of thinking. It is a considered point of view that delicately weighs both horror and circumstance, life and death, action and consequence, past and present, then crassly concludes that either someone is a "fucking idiot" or something is "horse shit."

Once, my mother's cousin Brad (the unofficial mayor of Egypt) rescued a distressed cow by shoving his entire arm inside the animal's birth canal to prevent its uterus from slipping out. It's a fatal complication for a cow having just birthed a calf, and a potential loss of income for a farmer. Arm deep in a cow's vagina, Brad instructed Mike (his son and my cousin) to take a jackknife and some twine and stitch the cow's vulva closed. Between each incision and sewing of the coarse thread, Brad inched his arm out while Mike vomited to the side. The cow was saved and a clearly traumatized Mike had experienced a gruesome rite of passage.

This story was performed over beers and shots of rye in the basement of my family home, which served as Egypt's unofficial tavern. (These were the type of gatherings where the mixture of Labatt and Crown Royal would cause grown men to order fifty baby turkeys then forget about it until boxes of freshly hatched poults were delivered to our front porch. It was drunken nights like these that resulted in us raising turkeys in our finished basement until they were old enough to be transferred to the barn.)

The fisting story killed.

"That's not funny!" one cousin snorted uncontrollably; it was the funniest thing they'd ever heard.

"Well, if you can't laugh at life's shit, then go kill yourself, eh?" howled another cousin.

In a world of common sense, where the golden rule was "don't put your foot in the thresher," life was rife with comedy. I was never privy to intellectual banter peppered with wit and bon mots, but to a bucket of harsh stories filled with obscenities, slopped and delivered with the cheer of a tole-painted duck wearing a lace bonnet and smoking the pipe of Jean-Paul Sartre. There is a tipping point to this type of humor, a danger that you might reveal too much. Learning to navigate this line was essential, because only by laughing at our situation were we given permission to complain, to express profound dissatisfaction, to show vulnerability, or to admit fear.

The world of Egypt seems lives away, but I am a farmer through and through. I eat when the harvest is bountiful, fast during droughts, and laugh in the face of hardship. While there is no going back, I remain tethered to the land. Nostalgia is in my blood.

When truth wades into darkness, I close my eyes. I am perched at the very top of a wagon piled with a hundred rectangular bales of straw. My sister and I are sitting side-by-side, laughing as the stack of interlocked bricks of compacted bedding sway dangerously to-and-fro, the coarse-but-sweet-smelling fibers sawing our bare legs red. We laugh as my grandfather looks back at us from his Massey Ferguson, making sure we haven't toppled off, as we chug towards the gray weathered barn. We squint at the horizon as the large black tractor wheels kick up dust and the late August sun burns bright, illuminating our world, making the ordinary, the simple, the nothingness appear anything but.

This was home.

STIFF COMPETITION
1994

Mr. Guy was my bald and surly grade eight teacher who used his class time to bemoan how the local Lions Club no longer permitted minstrel shows to be performed. He was an artist (and a bigot) at heart who enjoyed being theatrically lit by the overhead projector during his performative lessons. He was the type of teacher who only got into the profession to direct the school's "operetta" and the rest of the school year he peppered his lessons with off-color jokes and distasteful accents. Once, during his boring ramblings about Newfoundland, he reminded us to pay attention and enjoy what, for some of the thirteen- and fourteen-year-olds in the classroom, would be their last year of formal education.

As bleak as Mr. Guy's outlook was, his predictions were shockingly accurate. Expectations for success were exceeding low for a school built in the middle of a swamp. Our mascot was Skippy, a giant papier mâché swamp rat with a hobo stick. Morning Glory

Public School was a funnel for the surrounding concessions and dirt roads. Most "Swamp Rats" were from farms and small subdivisions, few were from affluent homes, some were First Nations from Georgina Island, but there was a high percentage of kids who came from abject poverty. These were the kids who lived in converted cottages, houses without siding, and trailers embedded in scrap-metal yards. For those kids, Mr. Guy kept a classroom pantry stocked with cans of Chef Boyardee and a microwave with a "no questions asked" policy.

The school bus was the great yellow equalizer. Every day started and ended with a forty-five-minute bus ride, and it provided a needed opportunity to socialize with our peers. Our journeys to and from school were always loud and out of control. Our bus driver Madeline Carpenter was a stout horse farmer with a round face, curly yarn hair, and aviator shades. She had a high threshold for the unruly, but daily she'd pull the bus onto the loose shoulder (nearly rolling it into the ditch), turn off the ignition, and arm herself with the emergency axe. "The next kid who sticks their arm out the window, I'm going to come back there with this axe and chop it off!"

The sight of a giant axe-wielding Cabbage Patch doll would make the entire bus fall dead silent. Then Madeline would return the axe to its resting place beside the stick shift, start the bus, and let the engine deafen the whimpers of traumatized kindergarteners and the stifled laughter of the grade eights in the back of the bus.

Public school seemed like a tedious journey to claim the back of the bus; a rite of passage as every September each grade moved a seat behind until they were ultimately ejected out the emergency exit. Graduation meant moving on to the only high school in the township, an even larger funnel with even more kids, and a seat once again in the front of the bus.

One morning during quiet study, Mr. Guy pulled me out of class using his trademark mime skills. He had marched furiously into the classroom (after being in the staff room for thirty minutes) and without saying a word he pointed at me with a courtroom accusation of guilt, made an umpire's circling *yeerrrr-outta-herrrre* motion, and banished me into the hallway. This signal was reserved for the bad seeds who set things on fire or hand-painted the washrooms with feces — the kids who smelled of woodsmoke and ate the free Beefaroni. I stood in the hallway for ten minutes until Mr. Guy appeared. A thick vein throbbed on his shiny forehead as he placed his two hairy-knuckled hands squarely on my shoulders.

I could feel my eyes beginning to twitch, my voice choke. I was always the kid who cried at the hint of authority.

This was not going to be good.

"Why did you drop out of the Lions Club vocal competition?" He began shaking me like he was acting in an after-school special. "Why! WHY!? WHY!!!! Every year you win!"

This was almost correct.

I had won the Sunderland Music Festival every year except twice: '87's devastating loss to Nick Harper, and '92's to some ringer who brought out a prop while singing the Canadian folksong "Squid Jiggin' Ground." (When that charlatan pulled out a handkerchief on the line "And if you get cranky without your silk *hanky*," I was furious.) That year I also won a landslide victory in the fall, becoming MGPS's first student council president to govern in a tracksuit and headgear. I cleaned up at the effective speaking competition with a loose ten-minute stump about my dirty bedroom. I beat Stacy Kaiser (the smartest and tallest girl in the school) and her snoozer about her family's vacation to PEI, then I continued on to dominate the regional circuit by creaming the competition. Stories about a tenacious Laura Secord and the legacy of Terry Fox were no match for a rousing tale of house cleaning and stain removal. I was the lead in all the school shows. I had the trophies, the badges, the plaques, the cash prize money, but what I didn't have was a solo in the town's figure skating carnival.

"I'm really focused on my figure-skating career right now, Mr. Guy. I just can't!" I broke out in tears.

I always had a career, never a hobby.

"Figure skating! You disappoint me." Mr. Guy did have admirable diction. "I've seen the results of your Scantron sheet. Your future is clearly as an actor, entertainer, or environmental scientist! Those were the results of your aptitude test."

"I know! I'm sorry!"

"Well, you're on thin ice with me. Now get back to your desk and think about what you've done."

As the Olympic torch relay crossed Canada, the 1988 Calgary Games had started a wave of nationwide pride that poured into our homes, filling our cupboards with Olympic gold-embossed goblets, collector's items from the Shell gas station. We cheered the Jamaican bobsled team, whooped as Elizabeth Manley rodeoed her way into the hearts of Canadians, and I remain adamant that all children born in 1989 were conceived to David Foster's rousing anthem "Can't You Feel It?"

A triple whammy of back-to-back games (Calgary, Albertville, Lillehammer) over six years introduced me to a type of male who expressed his strengths wearing sequins, pirate shirts, and form-fitting vests. I watched Brian Orser backflip his way to professional status, Kurt Browning become Canada's Gene Kelly, and a young Elvis Stojko amp up competition with quad jumps and mixed martial arts. For me, there was no cleaner form of expression, no better way to interpret the madness of the world, than on ice.

Doug Hall was the only other male figure skater at the Sutton Figure Skating Club; he also happened to have red hair just like me. Doug had an athletic build, attended a school program for advanced children, and was the son of a doctor. He was the purebred version of me: he was better disciplined, more muscular, and came from an entire family of gingers. He was unbeatable, and he reminded me of the uncomfortable dissonance that occurs when passion is failed by ability.

You can't fake it until you make it in figure skating.

"Yeah, but he skates like he has a stick up his ass," my mother consoled me after yet another devastating loss to Doug.

We had just finished performing our male solo programs. There was a lot at stake: the winner would not only get his name engraved on a trophy as Best Male Figure Skater of the Year, but he would also solo in the club's biennial carnival. Doug had nailed his tribute to 007 dressed as a James Bond, and I had flopped through *The Addams Family* theme song wearing purple spandex slacks and rainbow sequinned suspenders. I had hoped that the artistry of my finger snaps and suspender tugs would somehow cancel out two minutes of unintentional pratfalls.

When the judges announced the results, I was in second place.

In a competition of two people, second place is last place.

Gravity was not kind to me in 1994; my body was doing the exact opposite of all the other boys. As their muscles lengthened and voices dropped, they swapped their juvenile sweatsuits for *90210* jeans, Donnie Wahlberg hair, and Will Smith earrings. I went into full hibernation as my body ambitiously tested the stretch of jersey while stockpiling enough caloric energy for an entire precision ice-dancing team. The entire force of the universe was compressing me into "Big Red": a giant donut of flesh and orthodontics, topped with a fern of red hair.

Much of my weight gain was due to the fundraiser organized by the skating club to raise money for the carnival. That year every child was sent home with as many large boxes of overpriced chocolate-covered almonds and caramel bars as they could carry to sell to their neighbors. But we had no neighbors. My mother proudly displayed a Block Parent sign in the front window of our living room, but the red and white insignia proved as effective as a lighthouse in a desert. For years, the plastic square leaned against the glass, baking in the southern exposure until it eventually grew brittle and crumbled. Without anyone to guilt into buying an overpriced box of saturated fats, I tried to eat my way into being the top seller, inadvertently transforming myself into the world's first human Zamboni.

But Doug became my true nemesis, not just my main competition, after a wedge issue was driven between our mothers, and therefore us. Rehearsals for carnival had ignited a hot-button gender issue. Janet, Doug's mom, was furious that the grand finale to the superhero-themed event would be scored to Whitney Houston's "I'm Every Woman." *The Bodyguard* soundtrack was at the top of the charts, and since figure skating is the purest way to reinterpret the latest cultural phenomenon, it only seemed appropriate to end the show with the rousing popular feminist anthem.

"I will not have my *son* dancing to THAT song!" Mrs. Hall shouted at the gathering of skating moms at the emergency plenary session in the arena lobby. Janet stormed off, yanking Doug, still in his skates, out of the arena. "Well, at least we know where Doug gets the stick up his ass from," my mom snarked.

"You don't care about skating to that song, do you?" asked Marg Mercier, the president of the skating club (and the woman who created my colorful knit sweaters and sparkly Lycra outfits). "It would be an honor," I said, taking off an imaginary top hat and bowing for the mothers.

The first time I heard Whitney Houston's "I Wanna Dance with Somebody (Who Loves Me)," I was in the car with my mother and sister. Houston's voice soared on the radio, the syncopated enabling lyrics asked me to dance, begged for me to dance, then told me to dance. *DANCE!*

I needed to dance.

"And that was Whitney Houston's new single from her second studio album, *Whitney*," called the radio announcer.

I immediately committed the singer's name to memory.

Whitney. Whitney. Whitney. Whitney.

We were on one of our long quarterly journeys to Newmarket to stock up on some of the seasonal fashions at Zellers. My mother despised shopping. She held a natural aversion to spending money, and her "go without" attitude meant shopping with her was like haggling with a Turkish vendor. She preferred the peaceful convenience of the Sears catalog, plus the cheap dyes and stale air of a low-end department store always triggered my violent nosebleeds. With two kids and a tight budget, every visit to Newmarket ended in a temper tantrum and bloodshed.

As we passed the electronics section, I saw a cassette cover featuring a young black woman wearing a crisp white tank top against a gray background; her buoyant curly hair defied gravity. Centered at the top was a scratchy white cursive signature. With her thumb tucked into the fabric of her shirt, Whitney waved at me with a four-fingered hello.

"Mom, it's her!" I exclaimed.

My mother looked down at me with a *my-child's-an-asshole* look, and knowing exactly what was coming, she anchored her feet and reached slowly into her purse for a wad of tissues. Whitney was wrapped in cellophane, locked in an anti-theft cage, and labeled with a hefty price. If I were to free her, I would have to conjure the devil and end with a gusher. My mother is not a pushover when it comes to money, but she would buckle at the sight of blood.

I quickly willed myself to let blood, and a hemoglobin Old Faithful erupted from my nostrils in the electronics section of Zellers. My plan worked.

That night in the privacy of my bedroom, I unfolded the glossy azure insert and marveled at the autographed black-and-white glamor shot.

With love
Whitney

I clicked the black cassette into a gray office memo recorder and pressed play. The zipping sound of the sine wave sweep gave me a brief surge of nerves.

What was this force that I fought so hard and bled so much for?

Whitney would prove to be the first of many selfish battles as I reached the age of cassette: there was the hunger strike for Kylie's debut self-titled album, the vow of silence for Tiffany's *Hold an Old Friend's Hand*, the human air raid siren for Madonna's *Like a Prayer*. These were portals to an alternate universe manifested through foreign sound and images. An open window to a parallel world, igniting in me an innate force: if anyone tried to block my access, they would encounter a temper so fierce it rivalled a young Drew Barrymore in *Firestarter*. As technology became more affordable, so did the availability of the portals.

Bodley's Home Video provided a steady diet for my impressionable mind. It was a combo knitting and video store on the main street of Sutton, owned by an elderly couple. On the left side, Mrs. Bodley had a wall of yarn, patterns, and needles; on the right side, Mr. Bodley had a shag-carpeted wall and shelves filled with comedy, drama, and action movies. It was here that I wore out VHS copies of Whoopi Goldberg movies: *Jumpin' Jack Flash*; *The Color Purple*; *Ghost*; *Sister Act*; *Corrina, Corrina*. When my father purchased an antenna and router, we received an additional six channels depending on what cardinal direction the antenna faced. If we turned the dial to a southwest coordinate, our televisions went from black-and-white reruns of *I Love Lucy* and *The Andy Griffith Show* to *The Cosby Show*, *The Golden Girls*, *Designing Women*, *The Late Show with David Letterman*, and *The Fresh Prince of Bel-Air*. I saw a world opposite to everything I had learned, or seen, or overheard. The portals showed me a reflection of my deepest desires and directly contradicted my immediate surroundings.

———

"I'm Every Woman" was just a song (and a damn good one! *Chaka Khan!*).

Mrs. Hall could only see two boys clapping, jumping, and spinning to a song about female empowerment as slander against her son's sexuality. The arena was the town's central nervous system, and there was a clear division between the alpha hockey association and omega figure skating club. At the top of this chain was the Zamboni driver (the emperor of the rink) who would rev onto the ice and transform the space from a testosterone-fueled coliseum to a feminine, creative amphitheater. Doug and I were defying the natural order: boys don't figure skate in a small town.

At school, I hung out with the girls. (I had male friends but preferred what the girls did for fun.) I was the only boy in a group of tall girls who weren't necessarily cool, but they were smart and funny. I'd skip double dutch at recess, attend slumber parties (but never sleep over), and out of obligation we would slow dance together in the school's gymnasium. Our friendships would continue onto the ice, but the valued friendships I made with a few boys at school didn't translate into the arena. At school, I could make the boys laugh — even Justin McKimm (the coolest kid at school whose mom sold hot dogs while wearing a tube top outside the Beer Store in the summer). But on Friday nights, the boys I had sat with on the bus since kindergarten would walk right by me with their duffel bags and hockey sticks, flanked by their fathers. Even when I showboated in front of the glassed-in lobby with whatever rudimentary jump or spin I had mastered, I didn't exist to them. School was safe, but the arena was a microcosm of a society ruled by conformity, rigid gender roles, and competition, and we were children practicing — we fell and stood up over and over again while our parents watched.

The finale of the carnival was a grand spectacular, but only in the way a small town's Ice Capades could deliver. The industrial tungstens were replaced by follow spots and the entire arena seemed draped in Christmas lights. Doug and I took to the ice surrounded by twenty-five identically dressed Wonder Women. Doug was dressed as Batman. I was a fat Superman.

The entire town gathered to watch two young boys spin and leap to the one song from *The Bodyguard* that Mrs. Hall agreed to: "Queen of the Night." Maybe it was nervous energy, maybe it was the power of Houston's vocals, but I didn't fall once. I just grinned with absolute joy — gyrating, whirling, and clapping to the beat.

It was the last time I figure skated.

VOTED MOST LIKELY
TO BE STERILIZED

Is there anything more annoying than those viral videos of grown adults talking to their adolescent selves, spouting some gained wisdom?

The problem is that they are always from the perspective of someone who is highly successful. Someone who was short and now is a tall human rights lawyer, or the ugly kid who now looks like a swimsuit model and provides clean drinking water to villages throughout Africa.

Here are my words of advice to my younger self, as someone who took out the recycling this morning and threw it in the black garbage bin instead of the clearly marked blue bin.

Dear younger me,

Thoughts can kill. You will go to your cousin's wedding and see your high school bully and he will not have changed. At the age of twenty-nine, he'll still be an enormous (but attractive) asshole. After a brief encounter, you'll realize this and you'll whisper something to yourself like, "Fuck, just die already, you fucking-mother-fuck." Then a month later he will drop dead and you will spend several weeks believing you have psychic manifestation powers.

Dear younger me,
Fleetwood Mac is a great band. It's not just the music that your town's only orthodontist plays while torturing children. Your gums won't bleed every time you hear Christine McVie's distinct voice. A rogue braces wire won't poke through your cheek like it's a string from Lindsey Buckingham's guitar. "Rhiannon" isn't a warning that your diet will suddenly switch to pudding and mashed potatoes. *Rumours* is the name of an album, not a veiled threat by Dr. Hanser saying he's willing to tell the entire town that you have bad oral hygiene. And whatever you do, don't break down crying after you roll over your retainer with a desk chair in keyboarding class.

Dear younger me,
Never ever write a monologue in drama class from the perspective of a plantation slave. I know that you've watched *The Color Purple* compulsively

since 1985, and Whoopi Goldberg is your comedic inspiration, but that doesn't give you permission to write in what you imagine to be note-perfect vernacular. It doesn't matter that your teacher gave you an A+. No black slave working in a cotton field under the threat of death has ever stared at a tree branch and thought, "I remember apple pie." For millions of Americans, trees do not conjure fond memories of dessert. Please, whatever you do, don't give this monologue to the only black girl in your high school as a way of bonding. Just don't.

Dear younger me,
Bragging that you went to Yearbook Camp where you met other yearbook editors from across Ontario and made a yearbook about your time at Yearbook Camp is *not* a high-level status card. Nobody cares about "trapped white space" or the pica as a unit of measurement outside the context of Yearbook Camp. Also, don't tell that age-inappropriate blond joke to your uptight teacher on the car ride home from Yearbook Camp. You don't fully understand what it means, and she will be offended (but you tell it really well).

Dear younger me,
Puberty will hit very late. You don't need to go to the doctor every week and ask for a pill to "speed things up." There's no way to induce puberty;

just enjoy singing the role of Christine from
Phantom while you can.

Dear younger me,
The cafeteria lady is not your friend. Millie has a
gambling problem and comes to work after being
at Casino Rama all night. She's stealing chocolate
milk and rationing portion sizes of lasagna to the
students so that she can take home the leftovers
because she lost her paycheck to a slot machine.
Don't cover for her while she goes for a smoke; it
will set up a lifelong habit of doing other people's
work. Listen to her cure for insomnia because it
works. You can fall asleep while imagining you're
eating a giant head of iceberg lettuce.

Dear younger me,
Go a bit easier on your grade eleven math teacher.
She didn't realize that you would take it as a
challenge to flunk her course when she told you
on the first day that you weren't smart enough
to be in her class. She didn't know that you'd
use her class time as a study period for other
subjects; she didn't know how to react to your
mother calling her a "rich bitch" during parent/
teacher night; she didn't know that on your final
exam you'd leave the pages blank but write a note
saying, "You were right. I could fail. Just as you
predicted. But I was right too. You would fail to

teach." It's not your fault she transferred schools
the next year.

Dear younger me,
The cactus lamp you built in shop class is ugly.
Your mid-thirties homosexual self hates you
for it. It doesn't even look like a cactus. Don't
cry when you get a D on it, because you clearly
failed to capture what a saguaro cactus would
look like with a brass fixture and a sixty-watt bulb
crowning out of it. Accept the defeat and please
don't try to remake it to spite your teacher.

Dear younger me,
Your friend Jen will take you to the Upper Canada
Mall to get your haircut at Joseph's Coiffures.
A woman named Shauna will introduce you to
Joico hair products and texturizing scissors, and
she will give you the best haircut of your life.
Unfortunately, this means the end of your relationship with Debbie-To-The-Door, the woman who
has cut your hair in your mother's kitchen since
birth. When you feel bad about this, just remember
the time Debbie buzzed MC Hammer tramlines
into the sides of your hair that were an inch apart.

Dear younger me,
You don't have to unplug the stereo or any other
recording device in your bedroom before going

to sleep. You won't accidentally blurt out in your REM state that you are a giant homosexual, and it won't be automatically recorded by electronic equipment. (Similarly, you may also drink alcohol without fear of spilling the beans. Responsibly consuming alcohol will not cause you to blurt any of the keywords: homo, me, dick, oral, or gay.)

And finally . . .

Dear younger me,
Always remember this . . . it gets redder.

Yours Truly,
Future Shawn

I REMEMBER APPLE PIE

Nelly: Common weez gots ta keep on goin

Old Woman: I can't! I'm old. I've worked all my life. It's time for me to rest. My fingers are hard as dem rocks. I've bleed so many time cause dem cotton thorns. I can't go on..... leave me here. I'm tired and old. My saviour will take care of me.

I remember Apple pie. How my Momma would make it every Sunday. The taste, the smell of the house, every-thing. Never actually met him. My Daddy that is. Hang by some white men. I guess I'll meet him soon.

I thanks youz so much for helping me but at this rate you'z gonna get caught. Leave me! (angry) Leave me!! Nelly I'll tell your Momma that your a good kid & Your both good kids. I'm short on breath.

Look! There's a tree. I love to climb trees every step I take I get higher. What's that Momma? Come in for lunch. I'm commin. (hopeless) Every breath I take drains the life out of me. Shoot my shoes stuck! Help me Momma I'm stuck! (desperatly) Help me Momma I'm stuck. (weak) Help me Momma I'm stucl. The Suns so bright. Turn off the sun for me Nelly Make it so the bright rays won't pierce my eyes. Nelly! Nelly! Just Making sure. I'm so tierd. Look at thoes clouds so light and fluffy. I want to be there

I'm going to be there. laughing
Sweet Jesus take care of my soul.!
Let me be, Let me, gasp be (falls
gently to ground and dies)

Excellent   20/20

MY THEME SONG

My good friend Patrick wrote me an incredible theme song that I'm eternally grateful for. Patrick's inspiration for the piece happened while on a weekend trip to Montreal. We were in a four-star hipster restaurant when a well-intentioned server asked me, "How was your Brussels sprout salad?"

"Sulfurous," I replied.

It is an incredible honor to be someone's muse. (Until this point Annie Lennox's version of "A Whiter Shade of Pale" was my jam.) Patrick has created a relatable stinger that can be used to intro and outro a lot of my daily interactions and conversations.

The lyrics to the song are:

Con-fron-ta-tion-al Sha-wn!

You can sing it to any tune.

DAD JOKES
A SATURDAY MORNING SOMETIME
IN FEBRUARY 1994

My sister's grade-eight graduation dress was a black-and-white polka-dot tea-length dress with a sweetheart neckline and an incredible crinoline. The quest to find this particular dress was a three-month ordeal that led my mother and sister to the edge of Toronto, where it was purchased from the elite new Promenade Mall. After her graduation, a picture of Lori in the Dalmatian frock was framed and placed on top of the piano in the basement. The dress became a relic in the Smithsonian of her closet — a museum of wonders for a nosey little brother.

At times our family home felt like a rooming house of strangers in a Christopher Isherwood story, and I, the resident Sally Bowles, flopped in and out invading everyone's personal space: conflict was inevitable. My sister's bedroom was rich with interesting knick-knacks, tape cassettes, Baby-Sitters Club books, and hair products, but I needed a travel visa and a declaration of intent to enter.

Whenever my sister went out, I would immediately go into her room to look at the dress hanging in her closet. To feel the rough netting that caused the limp cotton-blend skirt to defy gravity.

It captivated me and beckoned me to feel pretty . . . *oh so pretty*.

The fit was entirely wrong for my underdeveloped thirteen-year-old body (also the high heels from my mother's closet didn't work, and I went a bit heavy with the blush), but when I spun, the fabric flared. I felt like Natalie Wood in her shortened confirmation dress teleporting to the dance through the magic of Technicolor just like I had seen on *Saturday Night at the Movies*.

I was mid-chaînés-turn when my dad, Ian, burst into the room.

"What the fuck are you doing?!" His left hand clutched the neckline of the dress and lifted me off the ground while his right arm cocked to strike.

"Take that shit off before I kick your ass, you little fa—"

He stopped. The word hesitated on his tongue.

"You hear me?"

He released his grip and I fell to the floor.

I cracked into a million tears. I had broken my own rule: don't get caught. At all times, I was aware of my father's exact coordinates in and around the house, always assessing his moods from any sound that emanated from the basement. Similarly, Ian policed the house from below by tracking my heavy footsteps on the hardwood floor. We were constantly clocking and predicting each other's actions. "Don't get caught" and "burn all evidence" were two rules I created after Ian discovered me making a columned list with *Boys I Like* on one side and *Girls I Like* on the other. The boys column listed any grade six, seven, or eight male who fulfilled the

Harrison Ford Factor. The girls column simply listed the girls I wanted to jump rope with at recess.

Dad stomped his foot between my legs as I spidered away. He stomped and stomped and stomped, backing me into a corner, until I assumed one of the various tight positions I had drilled. These were the fail-safes for when I didn't get into my bedroom with enough time to push the dresser in front of the door or execute a last-minute barricade by lying on the ground and pushing against the door with my feet until my knees locked. My father's strikes were always violent but brief — it was his surefire skill at shrinking me into a huddled mass that made me sob uncontrollably.

Every aggression he committed was followed by a muttered apology, an incoherent story about his father's woodshed, blackened eyes, and his asthma. There was an imprint of history with every contact, as if generations ago, a British man struck a child with such blunt force its impact reverberated through time. I was merely the endpoint of an assault that was passed from child to child to child, the heir to a legacy of normalized violence.

My parents gave birth to a nuclear plant of homosexuality, and they stared at me in absolute fear, not knowing how to remedy the situation. My dad wanted to cap it and risk all life being eviscerated within a fifty-kilometer radius, while my mother, Linda, wanted to vent it freely without obstruction. Linda didn't goad or champion my creative side; she instinctually knew that encouraging a gay child to express himself was like screaming at Niagara Falls, "More water! More mist! More whoosh!" I had no encouragement and yet somehow I spent my formative years dressed in spandex and sequins.

My father had suffered the embarrassment of a Cabbage Patch doll, the figure skating, the singing, the dancing, the Disney film references. On this Saturday morning, he decided to set a new course for the household, to end the blanket permission offered to a child who is an aberration. The verdict had been read. I didn't resist. The next morning, I put on my blue snowsuit, boots, and mitts and trudged outside with a lunchbox and a thermos of hot chocolate prepared by my mother. And in a cramped hut a kilometre off the frozen shore of Lake Simcoe, I would receive my actual punishment: ice fishing.

My father said nothing as I climbed into his truck. He said nothing as we drove to the lake and parked in front of Bonnie Boats Marina, where he stored his ATV. He said nothing as he attached the sled to his four-wheeler, loaded the gear onto the sled, and secured my helmet strap. He said nothing as we trekked several kilometers until the shoreline disappeared and we arrived at a tiny silver hut. He said nothing as he unlocked the hut, turned on the Coleman stove, and opened the floorboards. Nothing as he chipped the ice, scooped the shards with a pail, and discarded the chunks out the door; nothing as he baited the line with minnows. Not a word as he leaned back and glared at me while cracking the seal of a twenty-sixer of rye.

My father and I sat on benches separated by a luminous rectangle of frigid water. Outside, the wind rattled against the aluminum cladding, and underneath us the ice moaned as it shifted and cracked. The wooden rods bobbed up and down with the current, slowly marking time. The bright glow from the watery no man's land shadowed our faces ominously, and we stared at each other in silence. We were two magnets with north ends together, wanting to be close but repelled by an innate force.

It was a standoff and the only out was to concede or swim.

It was late in the afternoon when an old snowcoach rattled outside, and then an insulated glove banged against the aluminum door. A flood of blinding light poured in as a haloed shadow greeted us, "Hellooo!" It was Avery, a long-time family friend.

"Ian. Shawn. How are you guys doing out here?" He plunked himself beside my dad on the bench.

Read the room, Avery.

My father poured Avery a drink, and soon the hut was filled with gossip, fishing stories, and lewd jokes. I sat staring at the lines bobbing up and down like miniature oil wells, nursing my supply of hot chocolate while my father's bottle of whisky ran low.

"Hey Avery, guess what Shawn was up to last night," my father slurred.

"What?" *Avery, so innocent.*

"Go on, boy, tell him what you were doing."

"Dad, please don't," I begged.

"What happened?" Avery asked with a curious laugh.

"Go on! Tell Avery about your secret." Ian held up an invisible bell and rang it delicately — my father's universal signal for gay. *I would have gone with a more comical dick-eating gesture, but Dad always was a dreadful mime.*

"Please don't." My eyes welled.

"It's okay, Ian," Avery said. "I don't need to know."

"No. You need to hear this. Shawn got into Lori's closet and well . . ."

"STOP!"

From across the void I saw my father's fist threaten to strike. I immediately shut up. Shut down. I am rendered invisible. In horror, I watched my father reenact the details of the previous night for someone else's amusement.

I will not cry. I will not cry. I will not cry.

"Ian, it's getting late," Avery said. "We should get you off the ice."

"Fuck that. I'm just starting to have fun."

"No. Let's go."

Avery helped my father out of the hut and walked him towards the ATV. Ian drunkenly flopped onto the flatbed of the sled, his legs dangling off the back edge. Avery quickly closed up the hut and loaded our gear while my father drunkenly muled, "My son's a fag! My son's a fag! My son is a fag!" and laughed hysterically.

It took an entire bottle of Crown Royal for my father to be brave enough to voice his greatest fear. I had heard that word many times before from the kids at school, the hockey players at the arena, in movies. But hearing it from my father made me listen, and for the first time, I understood its meaning.

This is shame.

"Shawn, you're going to have to drive in to shore," Avery instructed. "Keep it in the lowest gear and follow the marked line. Go slow and avoid any Christmas trees. Trees mark open water."

Avery started the four-wheeler and pointed me towards shore. I drove slowly, following the path as the sun quickly started to set. Danger was everywhere. I could hear my father's incoherent cooing over the engine. I looked back at my father to make sure he hadn't fallen off the sled.

"My son's a fag!" My father confessed to the snowdrifts, the wind, the fishes gossiping below. "A fag!"

It's not my intention to grieve old wounds or embarrass my father, but to mark the time and place where Lake Simcoe took two victims that season: a father and son whose relationship would freeze from exposure, meld into the ice, and dissolve with the spring thaw. Our relationship lies in the silt and bedrock, preserved in the frigid waters waiting to be discovered. Years from now, divers will find the site, assemble the wreckage, and tell the tale of two anglers who couldn't handle the differences of their own nature.

MS HITCHINS

"Once you cross into the States, I want you to blow through every stop sign and traffic light," my father says.

"What?" I'm confused.

"You heard me. You cross into Buffalo, you hit the gas or else they'll steal the goddamn tires off the fucking Jeep."

There is no irony or sarcasm or self-awareness in his belligerence. If I could simply say "Okay!" and concede on compassionate grounds, the following scene would not play out as it always has, but I cannot tell my father that I am prepared to throw caution to the wind and ignore all U.S. traffic laws to avoid an imaginary group of auto-terrorist known as "they."

Two decades of Saturday nights watching COPS *on FOX29 has led to this moment.*

So instead, as I pack my mother's transfer chair into the hatchback, I say, "Are you fucking kidding me?"

"Just you wait," he warns. "You'll be on the side of the road with your mother and your aunt dead."

"Wait, I'm confused," I snark. "When do 'they' kill the women? Is it before or after 'they' hijack the car?"

"You don't listen, do you?"

"Well, if you're so concerned about the health and well-being of your own wife . . ." My voice cracks. "Why aren't you coming with us?"

A balloon of anxiety in my chest begins to swell.

"Fine, Craig." In the lexicon of the Hitchins family, being called "Craig" — my father's youngest brother's name — is a grave insult, a verbal snake bite.

The anxiety balloon threatens to explode through my chest.

"Oh shut the fuckin-shit-goddamn-up, the you two assholes." My mother has entered the garage.

Ravaged by MS, she reigns over the family with the bravado of a modern-day Richard III. Her right foot drags against the concrete as she limps toward us, grains of road salt cracking beneath her walker. My father and I watch this slow procession of horror in silence.

"Stop it, you twats!" she orders. "Quit being dick-nuts and help me get into the Jeep for fuckin-shit-sakes. This is my day!"

A crass ceasefire to the Winter Garage Conflict of 2013 is called.

The solution to world peace lies in one of my mother's multi-syllabic-hyphenated verbal smackdowns. In an alternate life, Linda Hitchins could have parachuted into war-torn countries and negotiated peace treaties with her hard-headed farmer talk. Any warlord or supreme leader or terrorist would buckle under her line of questioning: "Why you pig-dinks being such assholes? You've got nothing but shit for brains. Quit ruinin' it for everyone, eh?"

My mother swears more than she thinks she does. Our family has always been a pass-the-fucking-salt sort of kinfolk, and the way we communicate is peppered with foul language. A swear-jar policy was briefly enacted in our home, but my mother used the money to rent movies on weekends instead of donating it to charity and it only encouraged us to swear more. Her sailor mouth was how some semblance of peace was kept in our home, and she played (and continues to play) the unfair role of interpreter between me and my sister and referee between me and my father.

My father helps my mother into the passenger seat with great care. He grips her stiff foot and lifts her turgid legs into place by coercing her knees to bend.

"Your dad had the interior shampooed for the trip," she boasts. "Wasn't that nice of him?"

She is force-feeding me an opportunity to compliment my father and I have no choice but to bend to her will.

"The car smells like new. Thanks."

One must be stain-free when being carjacked on I-90.

Ian puts her walker into the back and shuts the hatch. Linda pulls the shoulder strap across her body and struggles to click the seatbelt buckle in place. I hop in the driver's seat and wind down the passenger window for parting words.

He leans into the interior and whispers, "Be careful, Linda. Love you."

"Love you too."

It's a tender moment between a long-married couple, and for a brief moment I see my father as a different man. I see my father the way friends and relatives see him, as the master electrician, the dependable hand, the able helper, the lovable prankster. The man I've been acquainted with but never befriended.

"Craig, blow through the lights — or else." He makes a throat-cutting action. *Ah, there's the dad I know.*

Ian's fears of what might happen to his wife over the next three days transform into aggression directed at the easiest target: me. Any hope for an acknowledgment of the responsibilities I've undertaken evaporates. I've lost again. We haven't even left the driveway and I am self-prescribing three recovery days in bed.

We drive west towards my aunt's house in silence. The blue Jeep chugs along the country side-road. The landscape is laden with a thick covering of ice and snow, the wind whisking the sheer dusting on the road ahead. Our silence is filled by the saccharine crooning of modern country music. It's been a while since I've last driven, and the Jeep's alignment causes the vehicle to constantly veer right. The vehicle should be traded in for a mobility van, but Linda refuses to upgrade; this car is the last bastion of her independence.

"The steering's shit on the car," Mom warns belatedly. "But your cousin Mike said that it was fine to drive."

"That's comforting."

"You okay?"

"Nope," I admit.

"I just don't get it. Never have. You two jerks are just not meant to be near each other, plain and simple."

Once again my emotional state has taken over the conversation. *This is her journey. We should be talking about her.*

"Yep," I say.

We pull into the gravel driveway of my aunt Debbie's gambrel-roof home in nearby Roches Point. The backdoor to the old Jeep Cherokee creaks open, letting a gust of frigid winter air into the warm interior of the car. My aunt Debbie slides onto the bench seat, her face eager.

"Look, Shawn!" Deb thrusts a metallic e-cigarette between the two front headrests. "Look what I got at the gas station. A thousand puffs! Do you think a thousand puffs is enough for me to get from here to Albany and back?"

Aunt Debbie is the world's most polite smoker. My grandfather Hitchins once told her "only prostitutes walk and smoke at the same time." Ever since, she strategically plans her smoking so that she is always sitting and never downwind of a non-smoker. After the roller coaster she's endured through the mental health-care system, no one in my family would deny her the comfort of a cigarette. She is overly conscious of her vice, and finding a way for her to have a steady stream of nicotine in the car and hotel room was key to her participation in this journey.

"Well, it's a fourteen-hundred-kilometer trip, so if you puff once every two kilometers you should be fine."

"Sounds like a good plan." She takes a drag from the metal tube; the tip flashes orange. She smokes methodically as if praying.

"It's got a battery-operated ember." She giggles as the odorless vapor pours from her mouth. "Isn't that cool?"

"That is cool, Deb!" my mother chimes in from the front passenger seat. "Isn't that cool, Shawn?"

"Yes. It is cool!" I echo obediently.

"Pretty damn neat, if you ask me!" Aunt Deb says.

"That is neat," my mother repeats. "Eh, Shawn? Pretty damn neat?"

"Yes. It is very neat."

We are all in agreement: electronic cigarettes are neat. This Curly, Larry, and Moe act set a parroting rhythm for the next seventy-two hours.

"Now, let's get the hell out of here," Mom declares.

With all the players buckled, and three passports accounted for, we begin the seven-hour drive to Albany, New York. My mother, like many multiple sclerosis patients, is taking a gamble on an experimental angioplasty procedure that will correct the narrowing of her chest and neck veins and hopefully alleviate some of the symptoms of her MS — a theory called chronic cerebrospinal venous insufficiency. The promise of a miracle cure discovered by Dr. Zamboni (yes, like the ice resurfacer) became her obsession, and a singular focus has seeped into her day-to-day conversations making them unbearable for even the most empathetic ear. Traveling abroad for a medical procedure not available to Canadians has the markings of a pilgrimage, and Linda has enlisted me and my aunt Deb to facilitate this journey. After two years of obsessing about this day, Mom is grinning in the face of uncertainty as we approach the Queenston–Lewiston Bridge.

"What are you smirking at, Mom?"

"Well, I'm excited. This is the first time I'm going to be in the good ol' U-S-of-A!"

"What? You've never been across the border?"

"Lin, you've never been across the border?" chuckles Deb.

"Well, only once," she amends. "Your dad said we could cross the bridge at Niagara Falls by foot but only if we were back before sundown. So we walked over, ate an early dinner as fast as we could, and were safely back in Canada well before dark — but that doesn't count."

I imagine this *Out-of-Towners* scenario as if my parents were played by Steve Martin and Goldie Hawn, and I burst into laughter.

"What's so funny about that?" she asks.

"What *isn't* funny about that?"

"I guess you're right! That is funny," Deb agrees from the back.

Linda has never expressed strong opinions on subjective matters. She is the product of a blunt Danish mother and a stubborn farmer, and these two temperaments form her personality: the stoic cheapskate or the practical warhorse. Although she is loving and affable by nature, you don't go to my mother looking to be coddled. Even if you are experiencing a major life crisis, you must clearly state that you are looking to be nurtured and not to be decimated by reality before talking to Linda Hitchins. This is why I started calling Linda by her first name for day-to-day conversations, and I reserve "mother" to indicate when I am looking for a compassionate ear.

Linda only comments on the immediate and important minutiae. Her daily phone reports communicate first and foremost who is dead and who's dying; followed by birth announcements, local petty crimes, and relatives with ailments; and wraps up with weather and a recap of the day's top deaths. Even on a slow news day, a conversation is likely to lead with a sensational *Uncle Grant Has Diverticulitis* or *The Sedores' Dog Got Rabies: Shot*. In the normal ways people express their personalities by sharing their basic likes or dislikes, she remains without opinion. She doesn't indulge in expressing her own desires. I know more about the intricacies of my relative's GI tracts than I do about my mother's partialities.

She has always said that — with the exception of a few questionable fashion choices (her exact words: "I don't understand your sweaters") — she has always known exactly who I was. I, on the other hand, have a sense of my mother only from the things she made, cleaned, or canned. The gradual deterioration of my mother's body means she's now unable to express herself through chores. Putting her faith in this surgery reveals a different side, and perhaps her newfound idealism is the only positive side effect of MS.

She is brave.

The blue Jeep chugs along the snow-dusted interstate as the winter wind attempts to sidecheck us into the next lane. I grip the steering wheel like an old sea captain. In the rearview mirror, I can see Aunt Debbie puffing away while tucking into a bag of sour gummy worms.

My aunt loves candy?

My mother's former dominance behind the wheel has made her a terrible passenger, and she sits with one extended foot working an invisible accelerator. Our car ride could be a poetic role reversal narrative for a movie of the week if my mother would allow it to be. Even though I explicitly volunteered to drive her (well before her decision was made) to Albany for the operation, Linda acts like Don Corleone detailing every instance of her generosity in my entire life. It's easier for her to claim my delinquency than to admit that she's lost the ability to drive and is now dependent on others.

I am bound to the mom-fia, and The Godmother has kept an itemized list of the thirty-three years she has been inconvenienced by me, and she is recalling her debt item by item.

"Remember the time that I drove you all the way down to the Hospital for Sick Kids?"

"That was for a hip operation because I had a tumor in my hipbone."

"I'm just sayin'. I did that for you."

"I was seventeen and still a minor under your care," I jab.

"I guess," she weighs. "Then every Hallowe'en I had to drive you around to go Trick-r-Treatin'."

"We had no neighbors!"

"I know. I'm just sayin'." She pauses. "Then I had to drive you all the way to Windsor so that you could audition for musical theater school."

"That was a terrible trip."

"Yeah, and you didn't even get accepted," she jabs back.

"Remember when you got drunk at your birthday party and forgot to put out the Easter candy? The next morning I came into your bedroom crying and dragging an empty basket." I laugh.

"Lin, you did not!" chimes in Aunt Debbie.

"She did! That's how I found out there was no Easter Bunny!"

"No!" says Aunt Deb.

"Yeah, I did do that." Mom giggles. "But who had to teach you how to drive?"

"You did," I say.

"That's right. I didn't get paid for that."

"Mom, remember what you said after I asked why you never warned me the tops of rhubarb were poisonous?"

She smirks. "Quit your bitchin'?"

"Exactly! Linda, quit your bitchin'." I laugh.

"Well, did you ever see me cook the tops? Bake them into a pie? Stew them into a jam? No. So you quit your bitchin'."

It was my mother who taught me not only how to drive, but also shave, throw a baseball, and plant a garden. I was branded a momma's boy early on, but my mother just picked up the slack for whatever undiagnosed disorder or trauma that prevented my father from being emotionally and physically accountable. Long-haul driving to skating competitions, university and college interviews, and day trips were all offloaded onto Linda, and my father would overcompensate for his absence by washing the car and making sure its fluids were changed. I was raised by women (by my mother, my grandma, my aunts, and female cousins), and years of little disappointments in my father's inability to be present has rendered me intolerant of any misstep he makes. Now, I consider my own failure to be present for Linda's day-to-day needs, and this counter-thought makes driving to Albany feel like tokenism — not the act of a son reciprocating years of dedicated support.

We pull into a Hilton Garden Inn just minutes away from the Albany airport and enter the world of destination medical travel at a four-star à-la-carte hotel. The front desk staff receive our check-in with the enthusiasm of teenage amusement park employees.

"I drove here from Canada to get my CSSVI procedure," announces Mom.

"Oh yeah, we get lots of those here." The clerk isn't interested in the recent business of hope that keeps the hotel rooms full; she is not aware of two years of circular conversations and saving money for a procedure that may not work.

My mother and aunt overcompliment the hotel rooms, hilariously ooo-ing and aww-ing at everything from the standard broadloom to the comfort of the mattresses. After an early dinner in the hotel lobby restaurant, Linda and Debbie fall asleep, and I indulge in the lax U.S. alcohol laws and sit in the hotel lobby, drinking a beer purchased from a soda fridge. It was an exhausting day of rolling my mother in and out of truck stops and repetitive conversations. I slip quietly into the hotel room and fall asleep to the seesawing of my aunt and mom snoring.

Please don't let this be my only family-vacation experience.

The next morning, with Mom admitted and prepped for the procedure, my aunt and I wait in the car in a medical strip-mall parking lot so that Deb can vape nervously in private. Even a routine procedure can bring out thoughts of the worst-case scenario. On rare occasions, my mother and I speculated on a future where she is not there to connect me with my immediate family, and my mind jumps back to that bleak possible future. Sitting in a frozen car, drinking weak coffee purchased from a run-down cafeteria decorated with an indoor picket fence and American flags, I am offered a hopeful glimpse of the future with my aunt. Debbie talks openly about the past (it's been her life's work to interpret and draw meaning from her traumas), and it's through her unguarded reflections that I have assembled a dark history of my father's family. She is the emotional archivist of the Hitchins family.

"Linda told me Ian went off on you before you left the house," she says between puffs. "You and your father, something is just not right there."

"I know."

"You know your dad never learned how to be a father because

Albert was cruel towards him. Dad thought Ian was weak and showed him no mercy. He got only one pair of shoes a year, didn't matter if he grew out of them or if they fell apart. One pair. Come August, he'd be wearing rubber boots in the dead heat. We were the poorest family in Sutton, but Ian *looked* poor. He had terrible asthma and the Sutton fire department would come to the house and give him oxygen, but that would only enrage your grandpa. He'd yell and yell and yell at him, as if it was Ian's fault. Then he'd drag him out to the woodshed." She takes a drag. "Linda and your grandpa Clarence saved him. Remember that, Shawn. God knows what he'd do, or any of us would do, without her."

I house only fragments of trivia surrounding my mother's past: I know that she won Miss Congeniality at the Miss Sutton Fair, she owned a yellow Ski-Doo, she dreamed of having a sewing room, she smoked until she met my father, she was teased because her father was the town poundkeeper. As my mother's disease advances, I have an intense need to discover and preserve who my mom was, but that seems contradictory to the reality of an illness that changes you daily and makes you accept the current moment. MS has unfairly become her identity, and my mother's natural hardness doesn't allow her to disclose her childhood ambitions, her first crush, or her disappointments with life. Now, when I ask her what she dreams of, she replies, "Walking."

The timer on my iPhone sounds: an hour has passed and we head back inside to greet Mom as she comes out of recovery. As we enter the cramped room, our collective fears switch to irrational hope and we have to temper our expectations that we'll find my mother standing upright and tap dancing in a medical gown. Instead, we find Linda lying on her back, rolling her ankles and wrists — testing for new sensations. If anything, her pallor is now a lovely pinkish tone.

"How was it, Lin?" asks Aunt Deb.

"It was nothing. I felt a pinch between my thighs and then a tingle in my throat."

"Well, there's always a first time for that sensation," I crack.

"That's not funny." My mom is laughing.

"Shawn!" says Aunt Deb.

"Well, if anything, I got a free pair of socks, a reusable tote, and a DVD of my procedure!" Mom holds up a medical-branded swag bag like it's a game-show consolation prize.

"Only in America," says Deb, a bit horrified.

We head back to the Hilton Garden Inn for one more night before venturing home. It's here, in an overpriced airport hotel room, that I have the extreme pleasure of introducing my mother and aunt to Chipotle. Even if my mom's procedure does nothing, witnessing two people eat a burrito for the first time is worth the drive to Albany. They dissect the flavors layer by layer, from the corn salsa to the barbacoa, and between each bite they take a moment to tune into their tastebuds before uncontrollably proclaiming, "God, that's fresh!" It is a rare occurrence when we as a trio are not trying to rectify the past or predict the future. We are simply enjoying each other's company by indulging in a burrito with guacamole (at an extra charge). Families are held together by smaller relationships, and these two women anchor me, prevent me from being estranged. A younger (more dramatic) Shawn might consider the line segments drawn between distant stars to shape a constellation and then relate them to familial ties. Now, I consider the humanitarian impact Chipotle has on the world while inhaling my meal and laughing with two of my favorite people, who (with sour cream on their faces) parrot each other between bites.

"God, that's light! Isn't it?"

Later that night, they fall asleep, and after I repeat the previous night's satisfactory lobby beer, I sneak into the room and once again listen to the seesaw snoring. But instead of sleeping, I stay awake listening for a change in the rhythm, making sure my mother is okay through the night.

The next morning, we check out of our hotel then head to a follow-up appointment where Mom is given permission to go home. There are no immediate results from the procedure (only time will tell), but for the first time in two years I have not heard my mother obsessively speak of Dr. Zamboni and his miracle cure.

Before pulling onto the interstate, I ask the car, "What do you want to listen to?"

"I like Jann Arden," says Aunt Debbie.

"I like Jann Arden," agrees Linda.

"I like Jann Arden!"

"That's good music," my mother declares.

"Yep, that's good music," confirms Deb.

"It is good music." I say, slipping *Living Under June* into the car's player. "Jann Arden it is!"

Seven hours of Jann Arden begins now.

FAILURE
(THE ORPHAN WITH PERSONALITY)

Success has lost its sheen since the advent of social media where anyone can frame eating a cupcake into a major life achievement. Here's the truth: your #cupcakelife is dreadfully boring (even though I'm liking all your photos).

I'm infinitely more interested in the person who will admit that while trying to bake a cupcake they accidentally replaced the sugar with salt, made the icing too runny, cut their esophagus on an eggshell, then discovered shortly after they were lactose intolerant. The person who can recount this experience in great detail with bits of chocolate sponge cake lodged in their gums (while their trailer burns down in the background because they unknowingly left their oven on full-blast) is my soulmate.

I'm the type of person who knocks on wood until my knuckles bleed and I contract an incurable staph infection. I'm a magnet for things going wrong. I know this because my mother reminds me almost every day on the phone.

"What can I say?" she soothes. "You've got shit luck. Never seen anyone just attract bullshit like you."

Success has many mothers, but failure is an orphan with a cold sore. For every high I reach, there is an equally deep low (if not deeper), and trying to establish a rock bottom is like watching a wildlife documentary about the ocean and feeling calm when the British narrator explains, "Much of the deep ocean remains unexplored; who knows the mystery of its depths?" At which point, I shout back at the screen, "Keep going, Attenborough! I'm a hundred leagues beneath you!"

My new favorite game is to clock how fast select individuals respond to my texts, emails, or phone calls. It's like checking my credit score, but for success. I know that if I email one particular person (let's call her "Mrs. X") for a simple catch-up and I have a really large project in the works, I immediately get an invite to dinner. But if I just did a public faceplant and email Mrs. X asking for coffee, then six months later I get an invite to her son's forty-five-dollar clarinet recital. These success verifiers are an instant and accurate gauge. Nurture these relationships so that once you do achieve your goals, you can intentionally mispronounce their names while entertaining them on your yacht (that has a hairline fracture in the hull and has drifted into pirate territory).

I get it. Nobody likes a cooler. I also get your playoff beards, and if I were flexible enough, I'd be blowing my own dice too. But failure, from what I've experienced, is just the inability to fit conveniently into an existing system. Like driving on black ice, you learn how to navigate it. You take your foot off the gas, you turn into the spin, stay calm, and whatever you do . . . don't hit the brakes. Does the first time nearly kill you? Yes. But your knack at walking away from future wreckages becomes a new measure of success.

Not dying becomes your luck!

For a while I befriended an American named Erv, this New York cabaret impresario who sported a fur bomber jacket on his visits to Toronto. We'd go out for dinner or drinks, then I'd help him navigate the internet to purchase bone shards of patron saints on eBay. He was a highly effeminate man who would screech out these one-liners that he'd been using for years (they were genuinely cutting and funny), and I would just listen to his stories about a pre–hip surgery Liza Minnelli and a post-stroke Bette Davis, while filtering out his hardcore Republican views, his problems with gout, and his shockingly bigoted statements. He was a tiny man who lived a large life and he wore his successes and failures alike as badges of honor (although they were hidden under the dead animals he shrouded himself in).

"Honey," Erv remarked, looking like a squat teddy bear. "If you're gonna fall, fall forward. At least you're going somewhere."

Then in the same breath, Erv capped off this erudite advice by saying something *really* racist, which in itself was a great example of failure.

From then on, we only talked about *True Blood*.

WHAT WOULD LIZA DO?

"Never idolize anyone alive," schooled an old drag queen. "They're human. You can only be disappointed with that very realization."

It was a welcome lesson on a rooftop bar in Provincetown, a conversation between strangers who had long idolized female celebrities. If there is one thing that can bridge an age gap between gay men, it's gossipy and salacious Hollywood yore. I ruminated on this conversation for years afterward, but the embedded wisdom remained stealth until I finally saw Liza Minnelli perform live at Roy Thomson Hall in 2011.

The sparkly chanteuse entered the half-filled space singing "Alexander's Ragtime Band." The term "living legend" seemed an oxymoron as she barreled through Berlin's century-old vaudeville hit. Gone was the phenomenon who exploded Giants Stadium with a defining performance of "New York, New York" in 1986; the marquee name who rescued the original Broadway production of *Chicago* after Gwen Verdon inhaled a feather in 1975; the leading lady who won an Oscar for *Cabaret* and an Emmy for *Liza with a Z* in 1973. During her short fifty-five-minute set, she pulled away from the mic on the high notes to mask her frayed vocal cords and her signature Fosse movements made me ponder the subtle difference between a jazz hand and a tremor.

It was the most human performance I've witnessed. She was frail: the icon cemented in the audience's minds clashed with the interruptive reality that stood (shakily) front and center. I quickly understood the general public's thirst for holograms and wished that at the eight o'clock curtain the house manager had announced, "Ladies and gentlemen, for this performance . . . the role of Liza Minnelli will be played by her official hologram. Please welcome 1980s Liza featuring her two original hips."

My fascination (bordering on obsession) with Liza began after I responsibly weaned myself off numbing antidepressants by flushing the entire bottle of pills down the toilet. The serotonin reuptake inhibitors had been prescribed by my hometown family doctor the summer between my first and second year of college as a stopgap until a permanent distance was created between me and my father. Flushing the pills was not the smartest move for a twenty-year-old prone to paralyzing anxiety attacks, but within weeks I found myself alone in Toronto experiencing every emotion simultaneously.

It was 2000: society had survived Y2K, and I had arrived in the city a child — underdeveloped, callow, and unprepared for urban life. Terrified of my new home, I would walk around with a takeaway cup of hot water, prepared to throw it in the face of a potential attacker. I left theater school to become an extra on *Queer as Folk*, and I pivoted my ambition to train as a contemporary jazz dancer (as one does). It seemed impossible to afford the three-hundred-dollar rent my mother was paying for a small bedroom in an artist house on Euclid Avenue.

I discovered Liza Minnelli while shopping at a used CD store in the Annex. I was flicking robotically through the rows of empty and chipped jewel cases when I found *Liza Minnelli at Carnegie Hall*. (If there is one pivotal moment I'd like featured in the film of my life, it's me discovering the essential live recording of Liza's record-breaking seventeen shows in 1987). Until this moment, for me Liza had been just a pop culture reference: the daughter of Judy Garland, the actress from *The Muppets Take Manhattan* with hair shaped like an upside-down pineapple. Curiosity made me purchase the CD and I was never the same again.

Hearing Minnelli sing had a more powerful effect than any antidepressants: the pills made me impenetrable, but the music rendered me invincible. Liza felt every lyric with unabashed emotion and unapologetic delivery, and her set list ran the gamut from the overly camp "Ring Them Bells" to the overly sincere "And the World Goes 'Round." Her voice was electric, a conduit of energy that eviscerated the sulking dulcet vocalizations and cryptic lyrics of artists like Sarah McLachlan and Natalie Merchant, the '90s artists who had fueled my teen angst. Liza's recordings directly paralleled my spectrum of emotions, and I immediately had a reason to get out of bed and carpe diva.

I began quoting her, mimicking her wishy, sibilant way of speaking, shoehorning the phrase "truly terrific, absh-olutely true" into everyday conversation. I landed my first talent agent by performing a one-minute impersonation of Liza Minnelli, which consisted of me screaming, "Momma! Momma! Momma!" around the agency office until they took me on. I learned the geography of Toronto by gathering materials to build a shrine to her. The city became a giant scavenger hunt as I ventured on foot, searching for posters, out-of-print biographies, VHS copies of *The Sterile Cuckoo* and *New York, New York*, and records of her many concerts and forays into popular music. I deciphered and memorized her oeuvre, interpreting these secular works as sacred. I began telling parables of her life to non-believers: The Parable of the Sally Bowles Haircut, The Parable of the First Homosexual Marriage, The Parable of Studio 54. When I felt lonely, I would turn on one of her live recordings, close my eyes, and be in a roaring congregation of thousands chanting, "*Liza! Liza! Liza!*"

In moments of profound doubt, I would ask, "What would Liza do?"

Yes. Say yes.

This new rule of thumb signaled the beginning of my blackout years, an extended rumspringa where I drank, danced, and fucked with the force of a million Minnellis. Propped up by a surrogate confidence, it was a hedonistic exploration that stopped just short of painting my fingernails green. My singular focus was to discover the things that brought me as much joy as Liza and then invest wholeheartedly.

Every week ended in the lineup to Buddies in Bad Times Theatre for Saturday nights in Tallulah's Cabaret. I would spend whatever money I had left that week, sometimes pooling cash with newfound club friends, to pay the five-dollar cover. Buddies was a catch-all for every representation of the community, and the goal was to get drunk enough off two-dollar Sour Puss shots to garner enough courage to stand on the cabaret stage. During the day, the stage was the pinnacle of gay performance, reserved for select actors in the city, but after hours it was an open dance space. On that stage, between bouncing to S Club 7, screaming to Spice Girls, and grinding to Madonna, I would take a moment to look out into the hazy, disco-ball-lit audience, and for the first time I could see the future.

I'm going to stand on this stage alone one day.

Aim a little higher, Shawn.

We were orphans, rejected by our families and navigating our sexualities blindly. Our mentors had been wiped out by a plague, and so we entered a precarious lifestyle rife with drugs, sex, and alcohol without guidance. The waning of the AIDS crisis and the approaching movement of legalized marriage created a spandrel, an unintended space. We were the placeholder generation: angry, afraid of sex, repressed by our circumstances, but we could sense equality in the distance. We were aware of our past, but selfishly wanted the ignorance that would be awarded to the next generation. We didn't know what else to do but dance and drink and wait.

The night wasn't complete if you didn't come home with your hair reeking of stale smoke and your clothes dotted with cigarette burns and soaked through with sweat and spilled drinks. It was an enculturation with considerable repercussions, and I find it remarkable that I emerged from this period completely unscathed. Absurdly, I thank Liza for my safe passage. (I know it's irrational, and as an atheist this is the closest I'll come to understanding blind faith.) In part, it's because I connected with a narrative of ambition, with a woman who once said in an interview with Barbara Walters, "I'll go out and sell walnuts rather than be depressed."

My infatuation with Liza propelled me through a difficult

period and I recognize the stereotype it made me, but I was no different than the husky kid who loved Nana Mouskouri, the effeminate twink who loved Dame Shirley Bassey, or the snarky hippie who loved Stevie Nicks. These were the patron saints of lost homosexuals whose life stories were borrowed as distractions from the dark and painful turns of our own.

I waited a decade to see Liza perform live. The disappointment I experienced was that I was unable to conceive that she was fallible, imperfect, struggling, and at times lost. I was upset that I could not blindly reciprocate the empathy, acceptance, and energy I so desperately sought as a kid. I felt challenged that my relationship to an artist could be a veiled act of consumerism made disposable with time. *Never idolize anyone alive. They're human. You can only be disappointed* with yourself *in that very realization*. And for that, Liza Minnelli, I am sorry. As one of your most ardent and unwavering fans, you mean more to me than a wobbly jazz hand and a few missing notes.

Now and then, I think about purging the remaining artifacts of my Liza Minnelli collection. I think about scattering the relics across the city, reintroducing them into the thrift shops and vintage stores for some young, impressionable homosexual to find. (It's a romantic idea considering everything is on the internet now.)

But I can't.

Not yet.

I don't know why, but whatever the reason I'm sure it will be truly terrific, absh-olutely true.

THE VISIBLE HORIZON

"Hey lady, is that your stash of Lean Cuisines in the freezer?" asks Varla Jean.

He stands in my doorway, wearing a pair of skimpy red bikini briefs, his broad, football-player frame filling the entrance.

"Pardon?" I lift my eyes from a dog-eared copy of *Alice's Adventures in Wonderland* that I found squished behind a dresser drawer when I moved in to the room.

I try to retain eye contact with Varla as he intentionally sandwiches his sizable bulge against the doorframe. I have come to observe this as a habit of many drag queens when not "in face": they spend most of their time shirtless and drawing attention to their crotches.

"Oh lady, you're crazy!" he cracks with his crunchy bilateral lisp. "So, the *Lean Cuisines* . . . in the freezer. Are they yours?"

"Nope. I wouldn't open that fridge even if I was wearing a hazmat suit."

"You crazy Canadian. I'm so hungry!" He voices as his drag character. "The last queen must have left them."

Varla's check-ins have become a nightly ritual since I moved into the Crack House, a dilapidated yellow flophouse for the various drag queens and seasonal workers of Provincetown. After a queen skipped town in the middle of the night, there was a town-wide reshuffling in the cabaret lineups. As various acts moved venues and accommodations, the B-Girlz were offered a six-week extension at the infamous Post Office Cabaret.

The B-Girlz was a trio of Toronto-based comedians who tapped into the North American pink market (pride festivals and cabarets in gay tourist destinations) — a difficult feat. The group was the creative child of Michael Boyuk and Mark Peacock, who created shows that combined medleys of pop music, sketch, and improv. Three zany color-coded characters (loosely modeled after *Golden Girls* archetypes) were the recognizable stars of these Glamor Disco Cabarets. Green was Hard Kora, the Bea Arthur type played by Michael; pink was Barbie-Q, the Betty White type played by Mark; blue was a revolving character played by a succession of performers after the Girlz lost their original Rue McClanahan.

After my agent called me with the audition notice, it took several long conversations to talk through what accepting a job of this nature would imply for a young performer. I had spent several years trying to break into Second City only to be turned away because I wasn't "dad enough." I tried stand-up but didn't feel welcome in clubs. I was beginning to write solo performance pieces that were getting good notices, but I couldn't break through. I wanted to work, and reality for most gay performers means wearing a dress at one point in their careers. The idea of getting paid to travel while collecting a good story was what kept me level as my closet filled with blue dresses I lugged (sometimes smuggled) into foreign countries and I became Ivana.

After accepting the extension of our run, the B-Girlz moved out of a single motel room on the edge of town. Michael and Mark settled into a cottage on the east end, and I moved into the newly vacated ground-level front bedroom of the Crack House.

The house's sunken foundation makes the entire structure lean towards the street, a quintessential Massachusetts murder home in the tradition of the Borden estate. The separating foundation meant the galley kitchen had become a gazebo with an '80s fridge and stove, a creeping vine growing through a one-inch gap between the two foundations. Emergency repairs have left trenches along floors, up walls, and across ceilings, exposing a geometric maze of verdigris tubing, wiring, and twisted joists. Upstairs, the bathroom is decorated with a lattice of black mold that originates from the grimy linoleum tile, creeps up the walls, and blossoms into a toxic canopy. It took hours scrubbing every surface with bleach, discovering ancient false eyelashes and exhuming fistfuls of Almond Joy wrappers sandwiched between my box spring and mattress to make the room livable. Every night, I close my eyes knowing that the entire structure could give out or the brown-stained claw-foot tub could come through the ceiling above my bed and kill me in my sleep. *But it's free.* Free accommodation in P-town during the summer warrants risking your life.

The hovel's neglectful owner is a hermit named Phyllis, a New York impresario who owns several businesses along Commercial

Street, including the Post Office Cabaret. According to local legend, she was stopped by the IRS while driving out of the Cape with hundreds of thousands of dollars in cash stuffed in her trunk and was put under house arrest for tax evasion. Allegedly. Since then, she's spent subsequent summers cooped up in her harborfront property with all the windows blacked out, monitoring her businesses through a live feed of multiple security cameras. Allegedly. Phyllis has an Orwellian presence in the town. Every show in the Post Office Cabaret begins with a phone call from Phyllis to the house manager asking about house size, and every show ends with a phone call giving notes to Michael and Mark about the performance. Her callous New York accent is mimicked by anyone who has taken her call — and anyone who has heard a Phyllis impression.[1]

I could dismiss the legend of Phyllis as small-town gossip, one among the many bizarre stories that results from flooding a small Portuguese-immigrant fishing village with homosexuals, lesbians with kids, drag queens, and gawking Midwest families. Mysterious fires and gruesome deaths are the lore of this town, and they contrast the jingoistic red, white, and blue Americana. With the bunting, flags, sunflowers, and saltwater taffy, Provincetown is a construct of the American dream and an apple-pie quilt for wealthy gay New Yorkers and Log-Cabin republicans from Boston who vacation in the quaint cottages and luxurious summer homes. For those who indulge in a short stint, the town is a playground, but as a seasonal entertainer, you thread between the oddball locals (who maintain the infrastructure year-round) and the reveling tourists and try not to get stitched up in either experience. You are there to make money and your only community is your competition — your fellow performers.

---

1   Allegedly.

Varla is the biggest act in town, and she fills the cabaret to standing-room-only capacity every night. There are two types of drag queens. First, the name entertainers (the magicians, stand-up comedians, singers, impressionists, and a capella acts) who play cabarets and theaters. Second, the female impersonators and pageant queens who lip-sync in bars and night clubs. Both wear dresses, but one is a remnant of vaudeville and the other a remnant of gay rights. Varla is the pinnacle of what it means to be a gay entertainer, an exceptional entrepreneur who sings, dances, and tells jokes while making an extraordinary amount of money. As much as we encourage ourselves in the daily slog of promoting and performing, a Rubbermaid juice container filled with urine reminds us of our place in the strata: we are underneath Varla's heel.

Varla's Piss Jar is a makeshift urinal in the cramped backstage of the Post Office Cabaret, a three-by-ten-foot space that houses wigs, costumes, and props for all the acts. The space is only accessible through the audience; a sparkly blue curtain hides this cramped reality where we do quick costume changes. It is said that Divine and Jimmy James and many other queer icons stood backstage here; their legend sticks like the booze-soaked carpeting. The rest of the cabaret looks like a cottage church, with exposed beams and pew seating; every pine-clad nook and cranny has been repurposed as food storage for the restaurant below — the elevated tech booth also houses dozens of flats of warm eggs, and backstage a broken freezer is filled with half-frozen French fries. This backspace is luxury compared to the janitorial closet we used in Puerto Vallarta to get ready in.

Varla's urine brews overnight and hovers above us the next day as Michael, Mark, and I apply makeup, latex, and glitter. The makeup process is a layer by layer ritual passed down from Michael and Mark. It begins with a close shave, blocking out your eyebrows, and a thick base sealed with powder. Furrowing your forehead to find the comedic eyebrow line, pouting the lips to find the perfect shape. Lining and shading in the areas with various shadows, highlighting the cheekbones and forehead with blush, then stippling massive amounts of glitter held in place with latex. The first time I got "in face," it took nearly two hours and we were forty-five minutes late for a tsunami benefit. Five months later, it has become second nature.

Barbie-Q is weighed down so much by the daily slog that she has started painting a smile on her face. Two little upturned hooks make her look like a glittery joker. Things have been tense ever since Hard Kora and Ivana were featured in a candid photo on the front page of the *New York Times Style* section and Barbie-Q wasn't. The article was titled "Rich Gay, Poor Gay." We are the photographic example of "poor gay" next to an image of a giant Cape Cod home. Hard Kora does her best to manage the contrast of our personalities, but even she is growing tired of playing mother between my suck-it-up attitude and Barbie-Q's sensitivity.

Holding stacks of flyers to distribute before the show, we roller-skate onto Commercial Street like three anime characters. We are greeted by Margie, a heavily medicated townie with a raccoon haircut. Margie acts as our part-time barker and stands outside the venue distributing flyers and selling tickets; she was also abducted by aliens.

"What the fuck took you girls so long? I've been out here for twenty-five minutes!" Margie shouts in her thick Boston accent. We greet her criticism with silence and a forced smile.

"What, you not talking to each other today, girls? Here, have one of my pills!" She reaches into her black fanny pack. Margie opens a tiny box to reveal a small pharmacy of pills, and she holds them up to her coke-bottle lenses and digs her thick finger through the trove. "I have no idea what pills do what, but the blue ones are amazing — fucking aliens."

The rule of thumb is that as long as the audience count is one more than the total number of people onstage, the show goes on. (Kids don't count.) One has to wonder how much damage Margie does pitching our show to tourists while slipping between her realities: the present, her running internal dialogue, and flashbacks from her space travels — all expressed outwardly in aggressive blurts. She's created an enemy out of Randy Roberts, a Miami-based singer who does remarkable impressions of Bette Midler, Joan Rivers, and Cher. Margie flips into anger each time Randy, dressed in an extra-short Bob Mackie replica, zooms by on a motorized scooter, flyering for her late-night show.

"Family show! Canadian comedy drag troupe. *Fucking stuck-up bitch don't take my flyer — think you're too good?* Family show! *Look at that bitch Randy Roberts stealing our audience. I see you* Randy *and your Cher-ass hanging out for everyone to see!* Direct from Canada! *Fuck you, Randy Roberts! Not fair.* Family show! See the B-Girlz before they're deported. *You never know when the bastards will take you.* Singing, dancing, high kicks!"

Arguments between acts are rare, but last week a squabble between two rival club queens resulted in the bomb squad being called in. The entire fudge district of Commercial Street was shut down as the Boston Police Special Operations Unit tackled a large suspicious cardboard box marked "die bitch" left at the entrance of an east-end venue. The town's pride flags flapped at alert red until the robotics team revealed the terror of its contents: a torn and tattered *Heart of Stone* wig stolen by one Cher impersonator and returned to its rightful owner (another Cher impersonator) as a threat. The incident is a reminder of how easily a sense of security is disrupted, but it's nothing that non-stop George Bush impressions can't fix: *Al-Qaeda hates our drag queens. Osama bin Laden hates gypsies, tramps, and thieves.*

We quickly skate away from Margie and down Commercial Street towards the west end. We roll past Ellie, the seventy-year-old transgender woman who croons karaoke Frank Sinatra in a bikini, past Dina Martina overheating in a spacesuit, past John Waters riding home from his day at the beach, past Michael Cunningham modeling a perfectly coiffed platinum-dyed haircut, past the struggling gay comedians trying to compete with the gimmicks of drag queens. Roller skating is the most pleasant part of flyering, and it's hard to believe at the beginning of the summer I struggled on the four-wheeled boots. Now we scull up and down the Commercial Street thoroughfare, handing out flyers and taking photos with strangers like amusement park mascots, because that's what we are. We are not real people, nor are we trying to be; our drag is one hundred percent acrylic: woven, spun, weaved, stitched, pinned, and set with hairspray.

We regroup in front of the venue for one last blitz before going inside. I roll towards a smiling woman walking in my direction. I present her with a flyer, and she throws her hand in my face so that the palm of her hand presses against my nose. "I feel sorry for you," she says in a dismissive tone before walking away laughing with her husband.

"I saw that," Margie yells back at the woman. "Fucking cunt!"

You can willfully fool yourself into believing your current and present situation is normal until you start agreeing with someone who has been probed by extraterrestrials. It's a turning point, that moment when something is no longer worth doing for the story. The sudden reminder that you are not an investigative journalist in your own life makes you begin to question the decisions that led to this moment.

I just wanted a job.

The audience for our seven o'clock show: four lesbians with non-countable children. The show goes on as scheduled.

At the end of a B-Girlz show, the stage looks like someone ransacked Phyllis Diller's closet: it is strewn with neon props, tear-away dresses, and doused with glitter. Blue glitter is embedded in my pores, in my gums, in my clothing. *I never want to see or eat glitter again.* Between the daily shaving and the wipes used to remove my makeup, my skin blisters after each show and my eyes water from pulling the latex off my eyelids and scrubbing the black liquid liner from between my blond lashes. We cram the entire show into three hockey bags and store them in the attic before leaving for the night. It's eight-thirty when we walk out of the cabaret and nobody looks at us or recognizes us anymore. It's a welcome feeling.

As Labor Day approaches, the nightly indulgences at the bar become routine; there is a natural and repetitive tide to the town social life that is only sustainable in short stints. As each weekend passes, you become less and less willing to be the rocks as the waves of tourists wash in and out from the shores. On my only day off since we arrived, I grab a sandwich and walk out to Pilgrims' Landing to catch the sunset.

As I pass a clothing shop, also owned by Phyllis, I hear my name shouted brittlely. Standing in her flowing dress and wide-brim sunhat is Ruth, my ninety-year-old housemate with a fused leg who works full-time at the store selling muscle shirts and designer underwear to gay men. Every morning before she leaves for work, she ducks her head through my doorway with an unlit cigarette wedged between the gap in her front teeth and states, "No time to talk today, Shawn! Such is the life of an artiste."

"Shawn!" she shouts. "Phyllis wishes to speak to you!"

"Me? Where?" I look around for a security camera on the street. "Right now?"

"Yes, she's waiting on the line." Ruth waves me in as best as her ancient body will allow her. "Use the phone by the cash register."

I walk through the store, past Michael, a tiny effeminate man with a rich southern drawl. Michael dreams of selling fine china, and he is also my least favorite roommate in the Crack House. One night he slipped in through my door with a catalog, crawled up on my bed like he was Maggie the Cat, and began obnoxiously describing every set and pattern until I politely shooed him out the door.

My heart is racing as I pick up the receiver and say hello to Phyllis for the first time.

"They say you got legs," a gruff voice rattles out of the receiver.

All the impressions are eerily accurate.

"Pardon?"

"Varla says you have great legs, you can dance, and that you're funny. That's high praise coming from her," she clarifies in annoyance.

"Oh wow. Thank you."

"I've been watching too, and I agree. Are you liking your accommodation at the Webster residence?"

"Yes, thank you for letting me stay there," I grovel. "It's wonderful."

"Well, keep it up," she says. "And you'll be back next summer."

"Thank you."

The phone clicks and I'm left listening to a dial tone. I stare at Michael and Ruth not knowing what just happened. I got out three thank-yous. *How Canadian.*

"Well . . ." presses Ruth. "What did she say?"

"She said" — I test out my firsthand Phyllis impression — "'You've got legs!'"

Ruth claps her hands in enjoyment. "Such is the life of the artiste!"

With a sandwich and two cans of beer in my bag, I walk out to the west end of Provincetown towards First Landing State Park. In 1620, the pilgrims spent five weeks exploring this area of Cape Cod but grew tired of its charm; they shipped off across the bay to settle in Plymouth. A tiny plaque that commemorates this event is hidden by overgrown beach roses and brush. I cross the breakwater, a long man-made span of rock that protects the harborfront from the shifting dunes. I lunge quickly from stone to stone as the tide begins to rush out. To my right, tanned and chiseled men wade through the salt tidal pool on their journey home from a long day at the beach.

That's where our audience is: the beach.

Jumping off the breakwater, I march in the twisting sand towards Wood End. I sit on a sweater and look out into the Cape with my back turned away from the monuments, the cabarets, the tourists. Alone at the edge of the new world, I am fooled by the uninterrupted line that divides water from sky. The curvature of the earth is undetectable, and I stupidly have to remind myself that the earth is not flat. This is only the visible horizon, and that too is an illusion. If I could rocket myself into sky, I could see the sun setting behind the earth's crust and bow spectacularly against the light. I close my eyes and dig my feet into the coarse mixture of sand and broken seashells. *I am now equal parts sand and glitter.*

Drag afforded me this opportunity. In the past four months, I have seen the sunset on the Pacific and Atlantic oceans, an experience I would have otherwise gone without. I enjoy this view because of the derelict artists, the aberrations, and non-conformists — the queer pilgrims who settled on these shores and instead of leaving, appropriated the local customs and created a safe place for like-minded individuals to gather and to celebrate. They built cabarets and bars and offered stages for gay expression that helped perpetuate an art form passed from generation to generation of male performers. If anything, the dress was an invitation to follow a path that had to be fought and won, and I was its ungrateful recipient.

This is the reality, but, like the horizon, I am too close to see this truth. All I can see is the dress.

With the tide, the land transforms itself hourly — a cycle of perpetual and predictable change. I slip off the breakwater and walk past the moored sailboats tilted on their axes. The bay of the harbor is exposed, and whatever rumors of a great white shark or Madonna floating in its waters prove false. The tide going out is Mother Nature's soothing way of saying, "See, honey, there are no monsters underneath the bed." As darkness sets in, the moonlight refracts off trickling tidal puddles and shades the grooves of the ripple marks. The otherworldliness of it all makes you consider the veracity of Margie's close-encounter claims. An arctic flow cools the night and the familiar crisp smell signals the end of summer. While plans are being made for white parties and word spreads about Hurricane Katrina off the Gulf Coast, I grow homesick for Ontario peaches, corn on the cob, and a mold-free bedroom.

"Lady, the Lean Cuisines!" interrupts Varla. "You're sure they aren't yours?"

"For sure," I say, looking up from my book. "They aren't mine."

"Good. I might eat them frozen, I'm so hungry." Varla lingers at the door awhile. "You okay, lady?"

I'm talking to Jeff for the first time.

"I'm okay. Just a bit confused by everything — but sad that it's almost over."

"It's hard here, especially the first year," says Jeff. "Lady, we live out of suitcases and half the contents belong to our alter egos. We go from playing opera houses one day to playing shitholes the next, and we never get to be our boy-selves. It's exhausting by the end of the summer. You'll be back next year. Till then, pull up your tights — we can see your lines. No one likes a mess."

"Thanks, Jeff."

"Now, if you'll excuse me" — he slips back into Varla — "I have some Lean Cuisines to gnaw on."

He closes the door, making sure his junk is the last thing

I see. Upstairs, Ruth is softly playing Glenn Miller on her record player. Her fused leg thumps on the floor, marking the downbeat in a three-four waltz. I imagine her reliving one of her many past lives through music. *Who is she? How did she end up living in the Crack House?*

I put my book on the bedside table and turn off the lamp.

ONE, two, three. ONE, two, three. ONE, two, three, Ruth thuds above me.

Before I fall asleep, I pray to the aliens. "Dear beings, if you're out there, don't let Ruth fall asleep with a lit menthol wedged between her front teeth. I don't want to experience the horror that becomes local legend in the great state of Massachusetts."

Such is the life of the artiste.

ALL HAIL THE RED, ORANGE, AND PALE!

With each dry-heave, my stomach violently attempts to detach, reverse itself, and eject into the toilet. My left hand knuckles the screwdriver needed to flush the broken toilet, while my right steadies my balance. A comet of sweat shoots across my forehead, my tongue arcs, and after a giant unproductive retch, my body collapses onto the floor. My face presses against the cold, dirty linoleum, and a long black hair curled in the adhesive gap between tiles dances against my rough exhalation. *Whose hair is this?* I try to focus on its movements, but I'm beyond meditation. If I were stricken with flu (better, a deadly plague that only a city like Edinburgh could germinate), I'd take comfort in knowing that thousands of others were experiencing similar fates. *Freedom riders? Race riot?* My stomach kicks, my body sweeps up like a goat marionette, and I bleat into the bowl. *Nothing.*

I leave the screwdriver by the porcelain base and crawl across a small landing to a single bed that lies frameless on the stained broadloom. I sausage my body onto the mattress and sink into its foaminess. I cloak my head by pulling the strings of my hooded black sweatshirt tight and tuck the scratchy blue-and-white kids' sheet up to my adult chin. I stare at the ringed, stained popcorn ceiling and appreciate the character of my hired flat. It feels authentic, as if I'm one hypodermic needle away from a *Trainspotting* experience.

The sun is rising on Edinburgh and morning is signaled by the screeching of the rough trade seagulls who commence their pterodactyl call and response. Through the cracked pane of my curtainless window, the steep roofs of the surrounding council buildings ignite with a vibrant warm glow. *Orange. Perhaps a sign?*

I am by nature a healthy balance of self-doubt and overconfidence, but for the first time uncertainty has clouded my outlook and possessed my body. *What were you thinking?* In this moment of profound anxiety, I sincerely regret tweeting weeks earlier:

> Just got official permission from Edinburgh
> council to host a Ginger Pride Walk on Aug 10,
> @edfringe! Details to follow! #gingernation

Within minutes of pressing Tweet, my simple post had been picked up by the British media, triggering a slew of Google Alerts in my inbox. The first and most alarming headline, published by the *Daily Record*, declared, "Militant Ginger Poet Stages Pride March." *Militant . . . maybe; poet . . . how dare they*. What started off as an innocent joke — marching hundreds of redheads through the streets of Edinburgh to protest "gingerism" — was now a Scottish hot topic.

I check the time on my out-of-date U.K. mobile phone. My index finger picks at the taped piece of paper on the back with a code that reads more like an algorithm than a telephone number. *How do they remember these numbers?* On my arrival, I went directly to the Virgin Mobile to purchase a SIM card and a ruddy young clerk looked at me and said in a deep brogue, "You're the man who's come to help save the gingers?" He grabbed a newspaper and showed me a full-page spread with a headline that confirmed his assumption. I thought once I landed in Scotland I would be able to control the momentum, but now I fear deportation. Last week, while distributing flyers on the Royal Mile, a Catholic priest approached me and said, "I like what you're doing with this affirmation march." He gave me two thumbs-up and I decided I'd seek political asylum in his sanctuary when this event turns into a bloodbath.

Four more hours until doom.

The dry-heaving began shortly after last night's show when a way-too-attractive man in the audience walked up to me and ruined everything with his Australian accent.

"Groy't show, mayt. Lee-sen, I down t'want to skee-er ya, baa't I herd wynd there wer baa-ses of gingees camin' up fram the bah-d'rs ta'arra, loyk free-dem royd-aahs."

"Buses of freedom riders?" I repeated.

"Ya, free-dem royd-aahs. I hope yewr ree-dee. Yew moi't stah't a ree-ce roy't."

"Start a race riot?"

I am petrified of authority — even a teenager holding a clip-board will trigger a full-fledged anxiety attack. My first (and only) speeding ticket resulted in a Xena-like police officer rubbing my back while I hyperventilated and cried behind the steering wheel.

93

I have been known to drive through roadside police checks one hundred percent sober, only to unexplainably start acting as if I just performed a barrage of keg stands at a bush party. But freedom riders? That's un-Canadian. Canadians don't invade a country and reenact the battle scene from *Braveheart*. No, we are invited to house parties, show up empty-handed, and eat all the appetizers, then apologize.

In 2011, when I first traveled to the Edinburgh Festival Fringe with an experimental cabaret that combined hyperbolic comedic monologues with jazz covers of pop songs, nothing could have prepared me for the scale of the festival. Imagine a haunted city built into a dead volcano infested with tens of thousands of needy jugglers, actors, singers, comedians, stilt walkers, buskers, university glee clubs, and Australians — all who are subsisting on a diet of meat pies, whisky, Red Bull, and zero sleep, all who are desperately seeking your attention. Every nook and cranny of the city is transformed into a makeshift performance space, and even with the influx of millions of tourists it is still incredibly difficult to get a patron through the door. On average, each act or show will have four punters in the audience.

The thick altruistic sheen of the festival masks an enormous industry that feeds off the resources of artists who not only pay astronomical presenting fees, but also bare the entire financial risk if their show flops — which many do. But Edinburgh can make your career, and the laureates associated with being a "fringe hit" are what drive relatively unknown talents to empty their coffers to wrap their faces on city bus ads with nonsense star ratings and pull quotes from university student bloggers.

For my first attempt, I did what every "expert" told me to do. I raised fourteen thousand dollars to fly a small crew from Toronto to Scotland. I hired out a small, tired conference room in the Carlton Hotel draped in theater blacks that had thirty seats and a lighting grid that hovered inches above my head. I rented a palatial Georgian flat from a Norwegian woman for my crew, their friends, and their friends' friends. I played by the rules and had four people in my house every night. I was a self-proclaimed Edinburgh flop.

I returned to Canada, deflated, angry, and embarrassed. It took some time before I could talk about the experience without being consumed by the immense guilt I felt to those who had donated money, as if their generosity had been contingent on my success. I felt as if my lackluster showing put me in arrears with some of my closest relations, and I was determined to rectify the situation. I would attempt Edinburgh again, but on my own terms, using my own funds. I made a two-year plan, and when I was offered a free one-hundred-and-twenty-seat venue in the heart of Edinburgh, I immediately accepted, making one promise to myself: go so big they can't ignore you.

The alarm on my mobile rings, and I've managed to get two hours of sleep. I un-sausage myself from the bed and slink towards the shower. At first, I had no idea how to turn it on. The shower presented itself like a Thorndike puzzle box. It looked like a regular shower but with a rotary phone dial and a pull rope hanging from the ceiling. For five days, I washed myself by squatting in the stream that flowed from the lower spout before I realized that the string and dial were connected.

I pull the string. I set the dial to seven.

Seven is a great setting.

My stomach unpretzels as the level-seven water warms my clenched muscles. By the end of August, without any additional support, I will have performed forty-four shows in twenty-five days and distributed over five thousand handbills to tourists. Two lengthy showers a day is my only indulgence. I towel off, quickly do my hair, and put on an annoyingly green branded T-shirt that reads "GINGER AND PROUD." I grab my knapsack, my black hooded sweatshirt, a dwarf British apple, and, after one last dry-heave over the toilet, I leave my comfy shack for the day.

My daily path cuts up Broughton, a busy street lined with independent flower shops, bars, and cafés ("café" means "deep fryer" in Scottish) inhabiting the eighteenth-century architecture that defines New Town. Edinburgh is a living cemetery where even the quaintest gift shop doubles as a monument to some epic battle or gruesome bloodbath. An acute sense of mortality pierces your North American arrogance; nothing here is permanent but the stones and the bones buried beneath. *If you aren't decapitated today, you can treat yourself to a plate of lasagna from the homosexual bistro with free Wi-Fi.* (The Scottish and I share a Garfield-like affinity for lasagna.) The dread entombed in the pit of my stomach prompts visions of medieval punishment, and as I round the bend of Leith Walk to face the Balmoral Hotel, my final destination, I am offered no stay or reprieve. I am about to be socially hanged, drawn, and quartered in front of the infamous British press. I am neither betrayed like Mary, Queen of Scots, nor am I brave like William Wallace; I am an unknown comedian who could not afford to wrap his face on a city bus. I am facing the career axeman.

Do it for the lasagna.

The green glow of my phone reads ten thirty when I arrive in the square at the foot of North Bridge and Princes Street. The usually scarce sun illuminates a panorama of Victorian and baronial architecture. *I should have worn sunscreen.* In the center of a square is an enormous bronzed statue of the Duke of Wellington triumphantly riding his horse Copenhagen. *This guy did something amazing to get his own beef dish.* The square is completely empty except for my publicists, Nicola, Dee, and Giles, and one unimpressed photographer from the *Daily Record*.

Nicola, an infinitely cool millennial with the voice of Nigella Lawson, has orchestrated this entire stunt. When "Ginger Pride" ballooned out of control, Dee, an experienced and forthright Irishwoman, stepped in to take the reins, and Giles, a preppy Matt Damon lookalike, is on hand for additional support. The three are laden with large posters on bamboo sticks, a megaphone, fluorescent vests, and bags filled with donated orange party wigs. We walk towards each other with nervous expressions.

"Are you excited?" Dee asks.

"I'll be excited when this is all over," I crank.

"Oh t'ank god. Me too," she admits. "Honestly, Shawn, this has been a lot."

Dee's candor and warm Irish lilt instantly calm me, and I understand that her reputation is equally on the line.

A brunette mother pushing a stroller wheels a surly looking baby with a head of fiery hair and porcelain skin towards us, and

Nicola makes the baby hold a hilarious handwritten cardboard sign that reads "DON'T MAKE ME ANGRY OR I'LL GINGER SNAP!"

"Well, at least we got one," laughs Nicola.

"This looks like a bust," says the photographer while snapping a quick photo.

I hate this asshole. *A bust? No one is coming.* I feel as if my entire career consists of throwing one birthday party after another and worrying that nobody will show up.

Dee leads me away from the non-action to do a quick hit with a local BBC crew that has arrived. During the interview, I'm not in my body; I'm saying things but I don't know if I'm talking out loud. *Am I even making sense?* I've become an expert for the entire ginger experience and I have absolutely no clue what I'm talking about. I finish the interview and turn back to assess the current situation. In my absence, a crowd of redheads has assembled and, in the distance, Scottish women with beautiful, flowing red locks, orange-haired children, two sets of twingers (twin-gingers), and even rust-colored dogs march towards the square.

I look to Dee. Dee looks to Giles. Giles looks to Nicola. Nicola looks to me. We all crack smiles.

"Bloody hell!" the asshole photographer calls in excitement. "This is something! You've got something here."

In the periphery, I see my biggest critic, a humorless American documentary filmmaker who's so deeply entrenched in the idea of ginger identity that it has rendered him unbearable. He's on site to observe — and, he would argue, to be a moral compass. Only days ago on his blog did he criticize my show for perpetuating ginger stereotypes, and now he's perched on the steps of the archives like a gargoyle, waiting for me to falter. I have drawn the ire of all the redheaded comedians at the festival, who are now acting as most comedians do when someone lands a bigger laugh — like complete assholes. Not surprisingly, they have all arrived on time and smiling, their publicists drooling at the fully formed swarm of paparazzi.

I'm pinballing between photographers and reporters when Dee directs me to a photo lineup with a hand-selected group of women. After we perform a series of ridiculous tableaus that are sure to haunt the internet for the rest of eternity, we join the crowd for a giant group photo. The photographers balance on the wrought-iron fence that divides the archive's steps from the square. The ginger gargoyle is forced to move.

It's now quarter past eleven and we have to start the march.

We never talked about how it moves.

Not a single person questioned the safety or objected to the stupidity of a North American leading a parade of people through busy and backwards European traffic. It is an absolute miracle that I haven't been mashed into the grill of a double-decker bus while navigating a crosswalk or roundabout. Nicola hands me the mega-phone and pushes me towards the curb. I wait for the lights to turn red as taxis and buses whip by, almost tugging pedestrians with them. The walk sign lights up, I take a deep breath, and my right foot steps off the curb. *I should have taken out liability insurance.* With the self-interest of a mother duck waddling across a four-lane highway with two hundred chicks, I move quickly and hope the mass follows. *If they make it, they make it.* I walk until I am beyond the protective shade offered by the Balmoral Hotel and into the sunny opening of the North Bridge. In front of me is a stunning panorama that begins with Arthur's Seat, tracks across the grand Carlton Hotel and tiers of medieval architecture, and ends with Edinburgh Castle. This just feels like my typical morning walk to the Royal Mile to flyer, until I remember that there is a small army behind me. I stop and look back to see Giles, in a hideous orange wig and fluorescent orange vest, holding up traffic, making sure everyone has crossed the intersection safely. He is a good duck.

As the frontman, the Pied Piper, I'm privy to two things. First, the panicked expressions of the pedestrians who are confronted by an oncoming swarm of redheads carrying signs while chanting, "What do we want? Sun cream! When do we want it? Now!" It is a sight that causes people to utter, "Oh my god!" Second, as we near the end of the five-hundred-and-fifty-foot span, I'm able to see that we have covered the entire west side of North Bridge.

The busy fringe crowd makes no attempt to separate as we snake up the Royal Mile, a noisy thoroughfare where performers pitch their shows to the unassuming tourists. We form a semicircle just south of the fringe gate on Bank Street and that's when I see two local police officers interacting and taking photos with an adorable redheaded toddler. Whatever anxiety that had tortured me with sleepless nights and dry-heaving seems so ridiculous now. It was just a joke, and it landed.

I see that everyone has a huge grin on their face, everyone is here for the right reason, and for a moment I feel that sense of community that is so ancient to me.

I make my way into the middle of the circle so that I am surrounded by people who look exactly as I do. I meet a strawberry teacher from Fife, the handsome twingers, a Canadian couple who made Ginger Pride signs in the first-class train coach. Everyone is bizarrely talking about their hair; even the men who have lost their hair are talking about their hair. (The barely legal twingers were explaining their engrossing theory about "how everyone has a bit of gay in them.") Other than a few improvised chants of "It Gets Redder" and a stump speech about bullying scripted by Nicola, I have no idea how to end what has become a giant hair photoshoot for paparazzi. *I should have organized ridiculous camp games where you throw eggs and water balloons at each other.*

I lift up the megaphone and announce, "Thanks, everyone! Let's grab a drink!"

Nicola pulls me aside. "Shawn, you're trending higher than Chris Brown in the U.K. right now. This is unbelievable."

I don't know how to process that I am getting more attention than an abusive recording artist with abs, other than with instant embarrassment. Like a cat darting from a litter box, I duck into an alley and begin to laugh so hard and so deeply that I take my sweater and jam it in my mouth to muffle any sound.

The conceit of theater is that it is somehow spontaneous, that "magic" happens when audience and performer miraculously connect. But it is a highly structured experience of rehearsed moments housed in a controlled environment and guarded by volunteers. An entire economy has developed around providing manufactured moments of human-to-human connection. I have spent most of my life inhabiting these dark spaces (as both a performer and audience), collecting these secular moments. They are brief and powerful windows into humanity, but occur so seldom that you begin to ration a single experience over a famine of bad theater.

An event of extraordinary luck has occurred: I have struck a geyser of energy, and its force scares me. It was a communal moment whereby complete strangers who felt constantly isolated because of something as simple as their hair color shared their experiences and felt a part of a community. It was something so spontaneous, so base, so unrehearsed, and I was at its epicenter.

This is theater.

I come back and Nicola is waiting for me with her boyfriend, Declan.

"Shawn, are you ready for this?" She grabs my arm. "We're going to the BBC."

"Is there time to grab a cup of Earl Grey?" I beg.

"Probably not."

We enter BBC Scotland. I'm now beginning to feel the exhaustion of the past two weeks set in, and I still have to flyer and shower before this evening's performance. I acquaint myself with the free coffee service and tap some instant coffee crystal into a Styrofoam paper cup before filling it with lukewarm water. Nicola and her boyfriend are celebrating today's success with some public displays of affection, and I close my eyes until further needed.

"Let me get you wired, lad," says a cheery technician.

He takes me up a staircase to a second-level studio. I sit on a stool, a green screen behind me and an ancient studio camera in front of me. Perched on the camera's lens is an upside-down Styrofoam cup with a smiley face drawn on it.

"Have you done this before?" asks the technician while weaving a microphone through my T-shirt.

"Nope."

"Don't worry, lad." He hands me a clear plastic ear monitor. "Just look at the smiley cup, and when the light turns red, try not to make a fool of yourself."

The technician leaves. Nicola and Declan settle in off-camera, and in my peripheral vision they begin to fully make out.

I must look like absolute shit right now. I'm wearing my mid-thigh jorts, a marketing T-shirt, and the black hoodie I've been sleeping in for about a week. I begin to panic and fix my hair. I hear a voice in my ear monitor.

The light turns on. I stare at the blue-pen smiley face. I talk and talk and talk until the red light goes off.

"Great, Shawn," says the mysterious voice. "That went to nineteen million people. Do you mind doing one more?"

"I'm sorry. Did you just say nineteen million people?" I squawk.

I can hear Nicola laugh off-camera.

The red light turns on. I stare at the cup. I talk and talk and talk and talk — *I'm not making any sense at all, mostly making up facts and statistics, I must look like a fool* — until the light goes off.

"Bang up job, Shawn," says a new voice. "That went out to sixty million viewers. Would you mind doing one more interview?"

"Did you just say sixty million viewers?"

I can hear Nicola laughing again. *This is an initiation.* I hear a new voice in my earpiece, a stately, trusted voice. I chat with the voice about where to find the best full breakfast in Edinburgh until the red light turns on, then I talk and talk and talk until the light turns off.

"Really great, Shawn, thank you," says a new voice. "Just to let you know that went to a hundred and ninety million viewers."

"Excuse me? Can you repeat that?"

"Yes, of course," says the voice. "That was BBC World Service, and it will air around the world to our syndicates, with a total reach of one hundred and ninety million people."

"So I probably can skip flyering for my show tonight?" I ask.

"I would say that is a safe bet," answers the voice.

Nicola breaks herself away from Declan's mouth. Together we have pulled off an incredible feat. I have an inkling that there will be a lineup down Cowgate for my show that evening, but I do not predict that the next morning nearly every newspaper in the U.K. will carry a full-page color spread or that Ginger Pride will be messaged around the world. Certainly, I have no clue that I will amass the most media attention in the seventy-year history of the Edinburgh Festival Fringe.

I suddenly feel very hungry.

"Anybody want lasagna?"

POST-THEATRICAL
STRESS DISORDER

It was the best of gigs:

My flight from Toronto to Victoria, British Columbia, was on time. I was greeted with a welcome bag of craft beer, trail mix, and fresh fruit. The technician was rested, skilled, and enjoyed my work. I didn't have to promote the show and the theater was packed. I received payment before I went onstage! There were no glitches during the performance. I had meaningful conversations with audience members after the show. I had four excellent sleeps in a premium hotel that offered a free cheese plate. The producers scheduled my flights to accommodate four extra days in Tofino. I drove through Canada's rainforest and turned thirty-four while watching the sunset with a group of German tourists.

I think about the experience often.

It was the worst of gigs:

Grease is a terrible film. It's dreadful, but not so horrendous that it deserves its cult following. The 1978 movie is the classic American story about a young Scientologist named Danny (John Travolta) who falls in love with an illegal alien named Sandy (Olivia Newton-John), and through the magic of song and dance they learn the universal truth that if people don't like who you are, you must change who you are. Then at the end of the film, the high-school sweethearts fly away in a stolen car while an all-white school of Protestants croon, jive, and wave goodbye.

Grease defines white people stuff.

My detestation of the film doesn't come from a one-time screening; decades of exposure to the cutesy, nostalgia-ridden film have morphed aversion into deep-seated hatred. Because of this brainwashing, I know all the punchlines, I can sing all the songs by rote, and I always triple-check my spelling when writing about the country of Greece.

A few years back, I received a fateful last-minute email from a booking agent asking me to fly into Winnipeg for a night to host a screening of *Sing-a-Long-a Grease* at a casino. Singalongs go against my natural instinct to be the center of attention, and I have just made my feelings about *Grease* quite clear (if not — it's *terrible*), but when you put these two things together, it's an easy paycheck. For a couple of years, I had hosted screenings of this program (along with *The Sound of Music*) across Ontario and solidified it as a consistent pick-up gig.

The job is simple. I'm the hype guy. I drive into a small town and warm up a packed audience with a twenty-minute set that mocks the film. I cue the technician to press play on the DVD player, the movie plays with karaoke lyrics superimposed on the screen, and the audience sings along. Meanwhile I sit backstage for an hour and fifty minutes, texting my friends until Sandy and Danny fly off, then I run out onstage and say, "Good night, [small town name]." I throw whatever chocolate almonds remain from my hospitality rider into a Tupperware container, hop in my rental car, and eat the chocolate almonds on the drive home. That's typically how the gig goes.

Cha-ching.

For this Winnipeg gig, I would fly in from Toronto in the early morning, stay overnight in a hotel, then fly out first thing the next morning. In less than twenty-four hours, I'd be back in my apartment watching Netflix.

Easy peasy.

I'm greeted at the Winnipeg airport by my personal driver, a lovely but exhausted man driving a black town car covered in gray duct tape. "Your limo is here, Mr. Kitchen!" He grabs my carry-on.

I am not particular about limousines, but my witchy sense tells me no good can come from driving around Winnipeg in a rotted-out town car. I roll down my window for some fresh air and within two minutes our car is illegally passed by an El Camino. As the car overtakes us, the man in the passenger seat (who is drinking a can of beer at ten o'clock in the morning) screams, "Go back to Toronto, you fucking douchebag!"

Charming.

As we pull in front of the above-ground parking lot / Radisson Hotel, the car is rushed by what I assume are fifteen extras from *The Walking Dead*.

"Don't mind them!" says my driver. "We have a bit of a home-less problem, but in the winter they freeze to death!"

"Wow! Is that so?" I react like I've been given the coordinates to an amazing local farmers' market.

My driver shoos the extras away from the car, reminds me of my call time, then speeds off down Portage Avenue. I check into the garage-hotel and spend the rest of my day catching up on sleep. When my alarm goes off, I hop out of bed completely dressed, pull my unpacked carry-on through the hotel lobby/parking lot entrance, exit past the zombified locals, and climb into the duct-taped limo.

The casino is situated in the industrial part of town, but it's hard to discern where the industrial part of Winnipeg begins and ends. At the train station–themed casino, I'm greeted backstage by a crew of professionals who have rigged the event using Joan Jett's setup from the previous night and decorated the auditorium to look like a 1950s sock hop. In the background, I can hear slot machines chiming in their ethereal tones. I feel instantly calm.

Everything is going to be okay.

My soundcheck takes exactly two minutes. I turn on my wire-less microphone, shout, "Hello, Winnipeg!" enthusiastically into the black mesh end, and confirm with the crew that the micro-phone does in fact work. Then I say, "Thank you, gentlemen, for your help. Before I go, did you play out the screener Paramount sent from beginning to end? Because sometimes it has issues."

"Yep-yes-mmm-hmm-ya-sure-did-absolutely," gruff the six technicians.

"Excellent!" I say, walking away. "I'm going to rest in the dressing room until you need me."

I'm sitting on the same couch where Joan Jett sat the night before, probably pondering her career trajectory, when there is a knock on my dressing room door. I find a nervous administrator standing in front of me. He introduces himself as the casino entertainment manager.

"Shawn, this is your five-minute call. We are sold out!" says the manager. I can hear the *Grease* soundtrack and the boisterous audience filing in.

"Great, congrats!" I say, ushering him into the dressing room. I open my luggage and reef out a shiny blue bomber jacket.

"Listen, before you go onstage, I need you to do me a favor."
Favors are never a good sign.
"Yes?"
"I need you to go out onstage eating a hot dog."
"Pardon?"
"You need to walk out onstage eating a hot dog," he repeats.
"I do?" *Where do my hired talents end and body rights begin? Also, am I contractually obligated to eat a hot dog?*
"Yes. Boss came into a load of hot dogs, and I need to get rid of them ASAP. I figure if the audience sees you eating a hot dog, they will suddenly realize that they want a hot dog."
"Hmm." *How do I get out of this?* "I see where you're going with this . . . What if I just point to the concession stand in the auditorium, more indicating to the hot dogs rather than ingesting them?"
"Boss really needs you to eat the hot dog. Chew it and swallow it."
"Chew it . . ."
"And swallow it," finishes the manager.

When a casino employee tells you "Boss came into a load of hot dogs," you should just accept this as your fate. And sure enough, just as I'm about to step onstage, the manager hands me not only a giant hot dog coated in mustard, but also a giant bag of popcorn.

"We need to push the popcorn as well."

I enter the stage carrying a microphone, a bag of popcorn, and this giant hot dog. The new props instantly throw off my established routine because: do I talk first then eat the hot dog? Or do I eat the hot dog then start my bit? I chose the latter.

I stand center stage in front of hundreds of drunk Winnipeggers dressed in lettermen sweaters and pink Frenchie wigs and without saying a word I bite into a giant sausage. I chew it for what seems like an eternity. I am not a fan of eating in front of one person, let alone in front of hundreds. I live in constant fear that I have bits of food in my teeth or sauce on my face. I swallow the garlicky meat (most likely consuming some poker player who was in arrears with the Boss), then take a fistful of popcorn and shove it in my mouth and chew it. Meanwhile, the audience is staring at me wondering what the hell is going on.

It is the most excruciating two minutes of my life.

I look towards the wings until I see the manager give me a thumbs-up, then I drop the food on the stage and dryly announce, "The casino wishes to remind you that they are selling popcorn and hot dogs at the concession stand." I take a beat to clear the kernels of corn from my throat. Then I shout, "Hello, Winnipeg!"

It's the most awkward opening I've ever given as a hype guy. I move on, turn on autopilot, and nail the warm-up. I leave stage with a boisterous audience who are really, really, really, really into rewatching *Grease* at an inflated ticket price.

I'm greeted in the wings by the manager, who hands me his

business card, saying, "Next time you want to play Winnipeg, you call me!"

I retire to the dressing room feeling Joan Jett successful, then I take off my blue jacket and set my iPhone for exactly one hour and forty minutes to give me exactly ten minutes to get re-ready to run across the stage shouting, "Goodnight, Winnipeg" before the end credits roll.

Halfway through my Captain Edward John Smith slumber, I hear a *Titanic* crash. *They didn't check the DVD!*

I run out of the dressing room and see the manager throwing his arms up to the sky, cursing the gods, while three technicians surround the video playback.

"Shawn," the manager says, twitching, "I need you to go out there and do ten minutes of whatever material you got."

"Okay," I assure him, "I'm here for when things go wrong . . . Not this wrong, but I got this."

So I walk onstage in front of hundreds of drunk people who were in the middle of the hand jive and begin to apologize, then attempt to lighten the mood with some of my best emergency hosting tricks. The audience is buying it — they're laughing along and taking the "intermission" to visit the concession stand. The hot dogs start selling. Shortly after, the movie begins to play, everyone cheers, and we're all best friends at Rydell High again.

I run off stage. The movie plays for fifteen minutes until there is another loud screech. The screen goes blue in the auditorium and the audience begins to jeer.

The manager runs towards me and says, "Okay, Shawn. Go out there and give me your best five minutes."

I only got ten, and I just gave them to you.

Once again, I go out and immediately start apologizing. I go into the audience and start cherry-picking people celebrating birthdays to sing "Happy Birthday" to. One at a time, birthday by birthday, to stretch it out. At one point, I catch myself saying, "Anybody here excited about Mother's Day tomorrow?"

The movie starts. I run off. I breathe. The movie stops. I gasp. I run on. I improvise. The movie starts. I run off. The movie stops. I run on. The movie starts. I run off. I'm like a one-man British farce, but each time this stop/start occurs the audience grows angrier and angrier.

The audience begins to boo, like a real boo. Like an earnest, you-fucking-suck boo.

I have only booed one performance in my life. It was Colm Wilkinson performing the role of Jean Valjean in *Les Misérables*. Mr. Wilkinson was singing the final note of "Bring Him Home," and he held the open "oh" sound in the word "home" for an impressive amount of time. As his air supply dwindled, he took a giant gasp and began singing the note again. Holding it for an *unnecessary* amount of time. It was so indulgent that I uncontrollably blurted "boo" at the stage. It was a loud and obnoxious boo that filled the quiet Princess of Wales Theatre as Valjean died. *And it got a great laugh.* (Later, I was horrified to realize that I had a giant piece of lettuce wedged in my gums the entire time. I have never booed anyone since.)

Grease starts up again, except the DVD jumps ahead to the drag-race scene. *We land in a Los Angeles river basin, where Danny races Greased Lightning against Crater Face for ownership papers after Kenickie is knocked unconscious after bending over to pick up a penny.*

Cha-Cha DiGregorio (the forty-year-old Catholic MILF) starts the race by holding up her neckerchief and dropping it. The entire audience goes crazy, as if they were on the sidelines with the T-Birds and the Pink Ladies. Danny's vehicle edges past Crater Face . . .

BOOM!

The playback system dies.

Dead.

Kaput.

An intense sense of dread sets in backstage; we collectively conclude that we are without a paddle.

Like casual sex, a gig is a good gig if you walk away not feeling cheapened or compromised. But just like casual sex, inevitably something horribly embarrassing will happen. The skill to muscle through whatever onstage fluke happens is the "magic gift" offered to a performer. We're like weather reporters covering hurricanes and tropical storms, sent into the eye of a Category 5 with nothing but a microphone and the hope of being compensated. You always survive, but these hurricane-like experiences have a way of developing into PTSD flashbacks. Vivid traumas that cause you to slap your forehead on the subway years later thinking, *Holy fuck, that happened.*

I'm lying in the fetal position when the manager walks over and says, "Shawn, I need you to finish it."

"Like, say goodnight?" I whimper with hope.

"No. I need you to finish the movie."

"Pardon me?"

"Go out there, maybe do some dialogue, and sing the last number." He says it with an eat-the-hot-dog tone.

And, because I fear how the casino came into a shipment of hot dogs, I go out on stage (one last time) and begin to improvise the final scenes of *Grease*. I re-enact the end of the drag race, Sandy arriving at the carnival, Danny and Sandy flying away in the car at the end. I start to sing "We Go Together," but I cannot remember the goddamn lyrics. The nonsense multisyllabic lyrics that have occupied valuable hard drive space in my brain are lost. So, I make them up:

> *Rama-tama-ka-linky-dinky-stink*
> *Shapa-tapa-clapa-ger-flapa-tapity-tonk*
> *Ganky-flanky-banky-shoobee-stop-a-stop*
> *Beans-o-danky-e-danky-donk!*
> *Greasy-fleecy-flea-boo-bop!*
> *Wooo!*

I do all this while an auditorium of five hundred intoxicated revelers scream, "You fucking suck!"

I do.

I do fucking suck.

If you're looking for the gates of hell, its threshold is in a Winnipeg casino where grown-ass adults dress like teenagers and eat an endless supply of hot dogs.

"Goodnight, Winnipeg!" I announce.

I run off stage. *Joan Jett didn't have to deal with this shit.* I grab my carry-on and head for the stage door. Flanked by four security guards, I am escorted to my duct-tape limousine that sits idling, waiting for my exit. They toss my bag in the back seat and advise me to lie low until we're out of the parking lot.

"Drive!" shouts one of the security guards, smacking the car like a horse.

My exhausted driver, who has no idea what has transpired inside, hits the gas and we burn away from the stage door. I peek over the duct-taped window ledge and see the audience stumbling angrily out of the casino looking for blood.

"Drive!" I plead. "Drive!"

As we breeze past the fake concrete palm trees flanking the entrance of the casino, my driver revs the engine and flames burst out of the dual exhaust pipes. I hop into the front seat and saddle up beside my driver, who throws his arms around me. The duct tape peels off the car, revealing a slick new paint job, and suddenly driver and I are dressed in tight black leather outfits. He squeezes me tight. "Ready, Mr. Kitchen?" he whispers in my ear. The car takes flight, and as we head towards the clouds I wave back to my newest and bestest friends.

"Bye, Winnipeg!"

I HATE MUSICALS

I was subject to the parenting practice that if you had a deeply effeminate child, you surrendered him humanely to a local community theater group, to be repurposed as an ensemble member in an exciting new production of *My Fair Lady*, *West Side Story*, or *Godspell*. Parents could sleep a little easier knowing that their irrationally gay son was blowing off steam dressed as a cockney gutter snipe, a gang member, or evangelical clown, his tendencies safely camouflaged by the *tra-la-las* of tone-deaf office workers, paramedics, and senior citizens that comprise a small-town theater troupe. This process ensured that within four years your son would not only have memorized the entire Broadway catalog, but would also completely dismiss a formal education — thereby saving parents tens of thousands of dollars in post-secondary tuition fees!

When I was fourteen, I walked into my high school lecture hall, a generous space with tired blue seating, pebbled concrete walls, and spaghetti acoustics. In the audience were the various teachers who taught drama (and English), dance (and French), music (and geography), art (and chemistry). Once I hit the center stage mark, I introduced myself, then broke out in an a cappella rendition of "Hakuna Matata" from *The Lion King*, voicing Timon's and Pumbaa's lyrics and dialogue. My best Nathan Lane secured a two-line singing role as the Salted Meat Seller in *Brigadoon*. When the casting was confirmed on the drama room door, I went home and told my father that I would not be able to attend my upcoming hunting classes due to scheduling conflicts.

Prior to this audition, I had spent Wednesday evenings and Saturday mornings in the wood-paneled basement of a bungalow in Keswick, Ontario. My father had paid three hundred dollars to enroll me in a firearms safety course. I was the only boy soprano in a chorus of ten or so irritated hunters (forced to take the course by new legislation) and one eager woman (who was a bit too Thelma for my Louise). We sat around two large folding tables while a balding firearms enthusiast taught us about velocity and bullet trajectory; the lineage of cannons to muzzleloaders to semiautomatics; the cleaning, maintenance, and safe handling of rifles and handguns. The final exam was part written and part practical. I barely passed; the instructor noted that I was visibly shaking while holding a semiautomatic pistol and suggested that I spend more of my spare time handling handguns.

I had never seen my father so proud. To celebrate, he unlocked his gun safe and we stood silently admiring his collection of rifles.

"Son, when I die . . ." he choked, "I want you to have my guns."

This moment looked a lot different in The Lion King.

Months later, that very pride drained from my father's face

as I ran downstage in a kilt, carrying oversized links of sausage made from papier-mâché and pantyhose. I could feel the spirit gum beneath my fake red sideburns pinch as I breathed deeply, but I lifted the weightless links of paper meat above my head and belted:

Salted meat I'm sellin' there!
At the fair, laddie!

I decided then and there I would become a musical theater superstar.

Anyone who suffers filing their income taxes as an entertainer has a similar story: the moment in which they caught the proverbial acting bug. But calling it a "bug" makes it sound innocuous or temporary, when in reality it is an invasive virus that infects a young host, commandeers its central nervous system, and forces it to grand jeté across a stage for attention. Whenever my career goes through a dry spell, even the most sympathetic ear will assign fault by saying, "Well, you chose this." It is a tough-love reminder that is entirely correct. Then I replay this salted-meat moment in great detail and remind myself that I was fourteen when I decided what my profession would be.

It was perfectly reasonable for a child to aspire to musical greatness in the '90s. The Toronto rivalry between Garth Drabinsky and Ed Mirvish was in full swing, and for the first time Canadian actors were center stage in Broadway musicals. Ontario was drunk on the mega-musical, and ornate velvet structures were constructed specifically to accommodate life-size showboats and helicopters. The greater Toronto area was inundated with prime-time commercials and splashy full-page color ads, propaganda archived on VHS tapes and posted on bedroom walls. There wasn't a single child in the province who went to bed without unconsciously hearing the Phantom of the Opera cackle: "Buy Phantom by phone: four-one-six . . . eight-seven-two . . . two-two . . . two-two."

School field trips were organized, musicals were embedded in the curriculum, and I learned who Elaine Stritch, Donny Osmond, and Diahann Carroll were from the very authorities who taught me English, math, and science.

I joined the local community theater and unknowingly entered a world of pancake foundation, jazz squares, and good intentions. The Queensville Players were a ragtag group whose mandate was to systematically shred the genius of celebrated twenty-first-century lyricists, composers, and choreographers, one Broadway musical at a time. The group was run by a handful of strong personalities with unplaceable British accents. In the basements of churches, these visionaries transformed white middle-aged farmers into Puerto Rican gang members and soccer moms into teenage virgins, resulting in stage productions that didn't just willingly suspend disbelief, they lynched it for paying audiences.

Community theater was rife with endless dressing-room dramas, showmances, and derailed marriages; it was a therapeutic forum for anyone experiencing an early, mid-, or late-life crisis. The Queensville Players was an all-ages group of weirdos who were doing what they loved most: ignoring their families to sing and dance in period costumes sewn from shower curtains.

I began living, eating, breathing, and sleeping musicals until I was a zealot. While other teens were experimenting with drugs and sex, I was taking my mother's credit card and driving to Toronto to secretly see Chita Rivera in *Chicago*. I skipped prom to learn how to hang and focus lights for the spring musical. I worked early mornings in the school cafeteria so that I could afford to take jazz and ballet classes after school. Every essay in my university preparatory courses argued that musical theater was an act of civil disobedience, or a universal language, or a catalyst for social and religious change. I imbued everything with a life-or-death rationale: *Gotta Sing! Gotta Dance!* I insulated myself with original cast recordings and souvenir programs and built a barricade from reality so enormous that not even the *Les Mis* chorus would attempt to scale it.

But my relationship to musical theater has deteriorated under careful examination over the last decade. A musical when executed correctly is an incredible feat, but most of the time it's just absolutely dreadful. I'm now ready to admit it: I hate musical theater. *Hate? That's a bit strong . . . You'd have to be a complete sociopath to not sob uncontrollably throughout* West Side Story *from the first timpani strike to the final gunshot*. Okay, fine. Specifically, I *dislike* musical theatre as a conduit for gay or queer expression.

My final musical audition was a callback for yet another Canadian production of *Anne of Green Gables*. I stopped mid–dance call and watched as a group of balding men jumped, leaped, and whooped, pretending to be school children. It was the same group who gleefully pretended to be cats or cowboys or Greek surfers. I watched them with an uneasy feeling, that same sense of discomfort I felt listening to gay men sing "As Long as He Needs Me" at fundraisers, or "I Dreamed a Dream" at piano bars, or the eye-rolling renditions of "Defying Gravity" at karaoke nights. Musical theater is built on the principle that when words fail, you have no other option but to sing or dance. I realized in that audition room that I was one of many young boys who learned to sing someone else's words instead of speaking his own truth.

Very few musical theater pieces are written specifically for gay audiences using a gay narrative. Historically, musicals were written by homosexuals who used heterosexual narratives for mass consumption. The ballads and uptempos sung by the female characters were reappropriated by gay men who decoded the ciphered lyrics and claimed them as their own. I firmly believe this cycle has prevented gay men from connecting with other gay male performers (and gay male vocalists) because we are not familiar with a direct mirroring of our experience and we are exhausted by constantly having to exhume our own narratives.

I am grateful for my early experiences — musical theater was a life preserver — but it has taken years to untwist my musical theater brain: to scrub away the saccharine and overly sincere interpretation of everything, to stop considering what I'm doing to be the most important thing in the world, to stop hugging and kissing everyone, to stop breaking out in song *in the middle of a sentence because I believed that was healthy attentioOoooooooOOn*, to stop muscling through terrible circumstances with a smile and a shot of cortisone because that's the price of show business.

Now, when I feel like I'm at a loss for words, or when I am brimming with compounded emotions, when that imaginary conductor's baton in my brain raises and the orchestra starts vamping, when that irrational impulse to sing takes hold . . .

I stop.

I take a breath.

I open my mouth and say exactly what is on my mind.

SWEATER ASSHOLES

I'm a terrible actor.

I have zero interest in playing anybody except myself.

I don't want to drop into a role, or walk in another person's shoes, or inhabit another's experience. (Unless it is a situation similar to *The Parent Trap* where I could switch places with a long lost identical twin to practice a passable dialect on a biological parent who abandoned me.) This is why I've had seven talent agents. Seven professionals who have exhausted themselves trying to wedge me into a system that I don't conveniently fit into. Very few roles are created for effeminate males with pink skin, orange hair, slight jaws, and high-pitched voices.

In Canada, the motto of most agents is to "throw a talent against the wall" and see "what sticks." This practice has forced me to tap dance (I don't know how to tap dance), boy band (I don't know how to boy band), and mascot (I don't know how to furry). I faked it until I made an ass of myself, and perhaps my greatest body of work could be assembled from the failed audition tapes that I wish I'd saved — they'd be an incredible anthology of humiliation.

I'm not a terrible actor per se, I'm just unable to play straight. I'm not believable in any role where a character identifies as heterosexual and whose sexual experience with a woman could conceivably go beyond heavy petting or erectile dysfunction. Gay men struggle in this industry simply because our natural state of being is deemed undesirable, which is problematic considering "a natural state of being" is the foundation of great acting.

Nobody wants to hear how hard this business is. Nobody cares. It is an industry that recognizes the few individuals who defy the odds, labels them a success, then paints everyone else as a failure. If I wanted a career where trying counts, I would have been an athlete. I would return to Canada with three Olympic bronze medals dangling around my neck, there would be a parade sponsored by Home Depot, and then I'd shout to the local news crews and fans, "I tried!"

But the business is hard.

Since I'm beyond the age of precociousness (*I'll never be a Disney teen star*), rocketing out of my years of idealism (*I'll never be a French underwear model*), and entering the realm of jadedness (*I'll probably land a podcast*), I believe I have enough battle experience to offer some sage wisdom to the young sissies breaking into this openly homophobic industry:

BEWARE THE SWEATER ASSHOLES!

A Sweater Asshole is the person in a creative or executive position who wears a comfy- and cozy-looking sweater made with soft yarns, fuzzy wools, and plush fleeces so that they can spout the most brutal and homophobic slurs while retaining a professional likability because they look so cuddly and cute in the sweater that Nana made. Although sweaters are a staple of everyone's wardrobe, here are four basic styles that indicate the presence of a Sweater Asshole: the Half-Zip Pullover, the Fleece-Lined Bro-Hoodie, the Himalayan Button-Up, and the Sheer Black Cardigan.

The Half-Zip Pullover is typically worn by heads of acting departments in professional theater schools. Do not be fooled by the faded black dye, worn cuffs, or the fact that he wears it every day. This is someone with a salaried (most likely tenured) position. This asshole will pull you into his dank office at the end of your first semester of theater school and alert you to an issue. He will draw a large imaginary circle around your entire body, pinpointing the root cause, then command you "to get rid of the gay." When you try to engage him in a discussion about practical ways to remedy your condition, he will simply state, "I don't know, it's not my problem. Thankfully, I'm not gay." You will drop out of the school weeks after this meeting, believing there is something intrinsically wrong with you.

The Fleece-Lined Bro-Hoodie is worn by directors trying to break out of shooting music videos and transition into more lucrative commercial work. While shooting all night in a Best Buy, this asshole will pull you into the DVD section and state, "You have gay hands!" Although there are many ways to say "expressive" (such as dramatic, exaggerated, or Italian), he will choose "gay." Then before you get two words into your Julia Sugarbaker stump speech about the Charter of Rights and Freedoms, he will point to his bisexual headset with his heterosexual hands and mouth like an

East German spy, "Ze client iz leestening." This asshole doesn't necessarily want to be the one to tell you of your obvious birth defect, but it's his first gig and he really needs the shoot to go well. You will bomb the gig. Your performance will be closer to a paranoid Lady Macbeth than a blue-shirt-and-khaki-wearing retail employee. You will go home exhausted and immediately Google "hand transplant."

The Himalayan Button-Up is worn everyday by the supervising producer on a single-cam comedy series. This asshole will give you unwanted feedback on an audition. Although the guest-star role was written with you in mind, she will find it necessary to state that "you're not commercially gay enough to play yourself on television." This will be devastating news. You will question: what does commercially gay mean? (It means the type of gay man who would shout "fabulous" at a supervising producer wearing a heinous Himalayan peace sweater that gives her a fucking wool triple chin.) Two months later, you'll watch a straight actor perform the best pinkface version of you like it was a goddamn Al Jolson biopic.

The Sheer Black Cardigan is worn by the deadliest of assholes: the executive with a background in accounting. This asshole starts every meeting by commenting on how cold the boardroom is while tugging at her lace-thin covering. She says nothing during a meeting. She is the last person to put her hand up to green-light your film-and-television development deal, but the first one to send you an email informing you that your contract has been terminated without cause or notice. *You will lose everything*. And, although she doesn't directly say anything homophobic, the follow-up messages from her coworkers fill her silence. This sweater asshole is the wolf in a literal sheep's clothing.

I have had an atypical career path because of these industry types; their ignorance only encouraged me to push forward through mind-numbing work, often out of spite. I know too many great actors, comedians, and performers who have given up simply because when their sexualities limited their work potential, they unfortunately didn't write their own material and fight to get it made. (I don't blame them.)

I always know to leave a working relationship with an agent when they utter in defeat, "I don't know what to do with you." (I don't blame them.)

I always know what do with myself. When I can't see any opportunity, I create one for myself. (Can you blame me?) Perhaps that's my actual talent.

FUCK 'EM

"Fuck 'em" was my favorite piece of advice from director George Bloomfield.

We were filming in the Distillery District (at the time Toronto's wasteland of film opportunity) in an old police station across from the Canary Diner. The derelict building had been favored by location scouts for years, and George could exhaustively rattle off a thousand different ways he used the iconic police interior and classic brick exterior over the past decades.

Today the basement of the building was transformed into an illegal exotic pet shop for a lame American series about family-friendly insurance fraud in Chicago. It was a cold November night shoot, and George had asked me to pull up his production vehicle next to the video village so that between setups he could sleep in the passenger seat. He was about to turn seventy-four; he was diabetic, had had two open-heart surgeries, and wore a locket of pills around his neck. On set, he had the surprising vibrancy of a student making his first short film — except during night shoots. The entire cast and crew took on the role of protecting him throughout the long and cold nights.

George was exhausted. He had gone head-to-head with a producer by the name of Denis Roberts, a bulldog of a man. Roberts was a spiteful on-set bully who was constantly barking against the clock, and his vileness manifested itself physically with a single herpes sore that circled the outside edges of his lip as if keeping time. It was Roberts who cornered me in the production-office kitchenette on my first day working as George's assistant.

"Did you suck cock to get this job?" he asked. "Are you a prostitute? 'Cause I wouldn't hire a fag like you unless you were sucking my dick."

Roberts was from a breed of old-school producers who used his influence and access to limited production resources to hire (alleged) strippers with cheap weaves and short skirts to answer his telephones. I was in the office for less than five minutes when Roberts accosted me, and for the rest of the season my presence on set was constantly undermined by him.

Television sets are not a welcome place for openly gay males (unless you're in wardrobe, or hair and makeup, or a high-ranking creative). Working for a director, like George, was intended as a shadowing position, an invitation to join the creative ranks reserved for ambitious young straight male directors. My presence on set was not only taking an opportunity from a "better qualified" individual, but also breaching an almost *don't ask, don't tell* mentality. As we neared the end of filming season one, George had grown tired of defending his gay assistant, and that night he'd spent his "lunch hour" arguing in Roberts's office instead of resting in his production trailer. It was a display of force that cemented the mythology of George Bloomfield as a powerful and unyielding director.

George was a legend with an encyclopedia's worth of life experience, and although fifty years separated our ages we were never short of things to talk about. In the rare moments where we had nothing to say, we spontaneously started improvising with a litany of f-bombs — trading and building on four-letter words like two jazz musicians. Most of the time, I would listen to him recount various anecdotes from his career, and at times I'd request my favorites like they were Nancy Drew titles: *Marlon Brando and the Case of the Fake Dog Shit*, *Bea Arthur and the Disappearing Bottle of Vodka*, *Ann-Margret Pukes on a Plane*, *Donald Sutherland Ruins a Feature Film*. His stories were proof that you rarely meet a celebrity at the peak of their career when they are receiving an Academy Award or a Golden Globe but instead in the low valleys of ambition before or after that moment — especially if said actor is shooting in Canada. Nobody recites the acceptance speeches, but they recount the temper tantrums, the manipulations, the addictions, and the egos.

That night, as George and I sat in the idling car to fight off the bitter cold, there was an unfamiliar silence.

I decided to force a moment. "George, why are you so nice to me? I don't understand it."

He held on to his answer, like I do when calculating whether I'm prepared to give an honest answer or shut everything down with sarcasm.

"Shawn, the world is filled with assholes, and I'm not one of them," he said bluntly. "People like Roberts . . . fuck 'em. Did I ever tell you about the time I fired Gary Busey?"

George had an amazing Gary Busey story.

———

The Bloomfield family had taken me in like a stray dog. I met Daccia, George's daughter, at a house party filled with porous Ontario College of Art + Design students, after drunkenly executing a cartwheel into the splits for her amusement. This was my elaborate wave (a conversation starter, really), which I spent most of my twenties performing. I hiked my leg over my head, tumbled, and contorted my body for the attention of complete strangers.

"You have to come to dinner with my parents!" Daccia declared.

And just like that, Daccia had unknowingly brought a wounded animal home.

Dinners around the Bloomfield table were vastly different from what I had previously experienced. At home, Sunday-night dinners were a hearty serving of leathered roast beef, mashed potatoes drowned in gravy, and limp broccoli cemented in cheese sauce. Meals commenced with my father picking up the two shakers in the middle of the table and blanketing his food in salt and pepper and ended with him dropping his fork and knife on the plate and walking away from the table. Monday through Saturday nights, I could eat in front of my TV in my bedroom, slumped over my plate on the floor, unknowingly devouring the Canadian television shows (*Fraggle Rock*, *E.N.G.*, *Due South*, *My Secret Identity*, *SCTV*) that George had directed. Sunday night was the only time

I was forced to sit at the table with my father, under his micro-
scope, where I endured a running critique of how I chewed my
food, held my fork, or slouched in my chair. I learned to eat fast (at
times choking on my food) trying not to draw his ire, but he was
relentless. It was the terrible dinner theater my mother and sister
endured.

There was no salt on the table at the Bloomfields'. That was
the first thing I noticed when I sat in their Victorian dining room
painted in Waterford blue and trimmed with large white crown
molding. Also, nobody asked for salt. The food was seasoned to
perfection by Daccia's mother, Louisa, an artist and chef who
hand-painted the walls of her home with surreal landscapes and
filled the spaces between with the most amazing food smells. I ate
fast, like a feral child, upon tasting avocado (served on the half
like a bowl and topped with cilantro, garlic, lime, and jalapeño
dressing) and roasted chicken with tarragon for the first time.

The Bloomfields talked about life and politics and religion and
art, and everyone at the table had their own perfectly crafted, hilarious anecdotes. There was familial history, and tales of Louisa's
and George's impoverished childhoods in Montreal added a sense
of provenance for the bounty of food that lay on their table. There
was no local gossip about who was cheating on whom with what
cousin, nobody was talking about guns or hunting, there were no
blanket statements or criticisms.

The first dinner I spent with the Bloomfields began at six thirty
in the evening with cocktails and ended six hours later with only
the traces of dessert left. Daccia had mentioned beforehand that if
George remained at the table, it was a good sign. George remained
seated the entire time. After that night, I returned weekly and kept

coming back over the next ten years, then every Thanksgiving, then Easter, then Christmas.

I learned how to eat slowly.

———

I had very few duties as George's assistant. I had to drive him to and from set, transfer his tiny hieroglyphic shot notes scribbled in the margins of his script onto any newly issued script pages, and remind him to take his pills. The rest of the time, I sat or stood beside him, carrying his leatherbound script, and observed him blocking the scenes.

He moved slowly around his actors like he was the camera, his two palms flanking his jaw, his index fingers and thumbs creating the lower part of a frame. For George, the performance always dictated the storytelling. I often witnessed him walk up to an actor struggling to deliver a performance and place his palm centimeters in front of their nose. "The camera is this close to your face. It sees everything. I just want you to know that." He would direct, and it would instantly turn around a performance. I know this firsthand, because he did it to me once while I was playing a UPS man on *Wild Card*. George had this habit of taking his assistants and giving them one-line bit parts as a joke. In this UPS scene, I was playing opposite Loretta Devine and I was so struck by the *Dreamgirls* star that I could barely deliver a two-word sentence. "Just stop grinning like an idiot," George whispered in my ear.

George refused to make a shot list or shoot unnecessary coverage to appease producers. He was constantly challenged by the continuity person or the director of photography for crossing the axis — an almost existential argument on any film set where various technicians argue about who has the better understanding of the editing process. "It's a matter of geography, not geometry," he'd school the crew, ending the conversation. He was always right, because he always cut in the camera. Years working as an editor during the founding years of the CBC allowed him to visualize how a sequence would be cut and assembled in post. He worked in reverse, shooting only what was needed, and this allowed for him to have a distinct signature that moved emotionally through a scene. He was different from the younger, more spry television directors who shot everything, assembled it in post, and allowed the editor and producers to shape their work.

While the crew was setting up or turning around a shot, the two of us would sit behind the monitors, making jokes and talking in weird voices, and George would recite some of his best stories. George would brag about how much weight he lost that week, how he went on a shopping spree at Abercrombie & Fitch one day and returned it all the next. It would also be the time when various background performers would come up and pay homage to George.

"Mr. Bloomfield, it has been an honor to work with you all these years," a career background performer groveled, waiting George's almost papal blessing.

"You too, darling. Really amazing work. Couldn't have done it without you," he'd compliment sincerely. Then, waving them goodbye, his face would comedically frown and with perfect timing he'd quip, "Who the fuck was that?"

Then I'd howl with laughter.

It was the tediously boring downtime that would prove to be

George's greatest lesson to me. We never fought, argued, or had a disagreement. Before his mentorship, I never felt comfortable sitting beside another man (father, uncle, cousin, boyfriend, partner, stranger on a subway). I was always calculating the underlying risk or the inherent danger, always waiting for it to turn violent or negative.

With my father, the only time that we could be alone together was when he'd watch '80s comedies and I'd hear laughter emanating from the basement. I would sneak down and sit at the foot of the couch and stare at the screen, watching *Police Academy*, *Coming to America*, *The Money Pit*, *What About Bob?*, *Caddyshack*, or *Uncle Buck*. Through Eddie Murphy, Rodney Dangerfield, Bill Murray, and John Candy, I was able to relate to my father as someone who could laugh hard and honestly, and the peace these comedians provided our household was welcome. George became a continuation of this comfort, and without him I would have never began a reconciliation process with my father, never learned to sit next to a partner without feeling the need to entertain, and never developed a trusted group of close male friends.

Oh, and George had a great John Candy and rib-dinner story.

On set, George used to joke that if he died during the middle of a shoot, the exhausted crew should go home and take the day off, on him. "Just so you all know, the show doesn't go on if I croak!"

When George died in 2011, four years after retiring, everything stopped. I didn't know how to label our decade-long relationship: mentor, surrogate, passenger, friend. I received condolences from friends and colleagues (even my own parents) who called or wrote to say, "I'm sorry that you lost your George." I didn't know how to qualify the loss I was experiencing, and for the first time I had to negotiate with grief, trying to rationalize loss as if it were a solvable algebraic equation where the sum of permissible feelings would be derived by the number of dinners at the Bloomfields' multiplied by the number of hours spent on set.

The Bloomfields became very much my family: Louisa set a place for me when I had no table to sit at; George created a place for me on set when there wasn't any opportunity. For years, we joked that I was the redheaded faux-son of George Bloomfield, and that was exactly how it was printed in his obituary.

Jokes always have a way of manifesting themselves into reality.

A few days before he died, George phoned me up just to say hello, as he did every now and then since he'd retired. "Shawn, I'm out of the hospital. We're barbecuing on the patio with Daccia and Louisa. It's a beautiful day." He had a rattle in his voice. He had been in and out of the hospital over the last six months as doctors fiddled with his medication levels. It was an entirely innocuous catch-up conversation that ended with a promise to see each other on Sunday. But there was a tone to his voice that triggered my witchy sense, and after I hung up the phone, I looked at Matthew, my partner, who had been half-listening to my side of the conversation.

"What's that look?" Matt asked, buzzing around the apartment, planning his impending move in.

"I think George just called to say goodbye."

"No! Don't be silly." He fluffed it off. "Don't think that way."

The phone call was a beautiful way to end our friendship.

On George's last shoot, he was beginning to lose his luster, and my role at times verged on caregiver and part-time storyteller. I clocked his health while prompting plot points and proper nouns, filling in the minutia of his trademark anecdotes that I had committed to memory. But, as much fun as a free luxury production car was, I was growing restless watching others work, and I became maybe a bit too lax in my attention. One day after lunch — where George had cut me a piece of cheesecake from the catering table and watched me eat it . . . he liked to watch me eat the foods he wasn't allowed — we all filed to set except for George.

"Where's George?" asked the first assistant director. As if I had only one job to do, and I'd failed at it miserably. I had lost the director.

Then there was a quiet but frantic building-wide search to find George Bloomfield.

George had wandered onto the empty stage beside the one we were shooting on. When I found him, he was lit by a single industrial work light, in a circle of white on the paint-stained concrete floors. He stood in the center of the light, costumed head to toe in Abercrombie & Fitch, looking around at the empty darkness and hollering, "What the fuck is going on here? Where's my set . . . my cast? Hello?!"

I ran across the soundstage as he slowly circumnavigated in confusion, arguing with the blackness.

"Where the fuck is everybody? Where's my crew?"

I visualized how I would shoot this scene in the style of George.

> *A long uninterrupted Steadicam shot tracks the geography of the hero. The hero demands answers from the space. The frame counters his moves until landing in a perfectly timed over-the-shoulder shot. Cut to: an obligatory shot (on a long lens) capturing Assistant's*

entrance into the foot of the light [unnecessary but establishes enough geography to shut up the continuity person]. Herein: we cut back and forth on a medium until opening up and pulling back to a movement that resolves the tension. The entire sequence is scored to classical music, most likely Mozart.

"George?" I say, a bit winded by the day's cheesecake.

"What's going on here? Where the fuck is everybody?"

"They're all waiting for you next door. You're on the wrong stage."

"I am?"

"Yeah. You went right instead of left from the bathroom."

"And they're all waiting for me?"

"Yep."

"Good!" He smirked. "Fuck 'em."

FK / LW

A friend once told me a story about her brother buying an ugly painting at an auction for ten dollars, not because he appreciated the work but because it "felt heavy" when he lifted the piece during the preview. When he got home, he dismantled the frame and found ten thousand dollars in cash hidden between the canvas and the wooden backing. She told me this tale thinking, "Shawn will really love this story, he loves treasure!" But my reaction wasn't "Oh wow! That's great for your brother. What a story!" It was "Oh, go fuck your brother. I hate him!"

I will applaud your award, your pay raise, your superhuman achievements in humanity, but boasting about how you or someone you know discovered treasure: braggart beware. I have learned to combat and work through my jealousy, but I am *infinitely* resentful of those who just happen to find treasure. Whether it is a Jackson Pollock in a garage, a hoard of Roman gold buried in the British moors, or a salsa sombrero bowl at a yard sale, finding treasure is my number one goal in life, and my ongoing inability to inadvertently stumble upon a major jackpot is a growing disappointment.

I am not confessing a desire to become a career treasure hunter, although I do see a safari hat and a metal detector in my retirement. I've obsessively watched *The Goonies*, all the Indiana Jones movies, and *Pirates of the Caribbean*, so I know that I'm unwilling to commit to unearthing local legend to save my childhood home, or risk my life fighting Nazis for archeological glory and the love of Kim Basinger. However, my inner pirate would easily slit a throat for a dime on the sidewalk, and recognizing that thirst scares me. GPS and X-ray technologies have completely demystified the act of seeking treasure, and that's not how I want it to happen for me. I want it to be accidental and because of the negligence of an original owner. If I had to get a badass prison tattoo across my chest (or face), it would read in large ornate script *Inuentoribus Custodientes, Victos Flentium* — Finders Keepers, Losers Weepers. FK / LW is how I navigate my day-to-day life as an active hunter, looking for something of value with no obligation to give it back because someone was stupid enough to lose it or sell it (wedding rings, pets, and children may or may not be exempt from this rule); this is my guiding moral compass.

My apartment is a trove of layman finds scavenged from sidewalks, estate sales, and Sunday markets. Everything has a provenance, and explaining with great detail how each and every object came into my possession is one of my most tedious qualities. I happily shame friends with my collection of mid-century furniture, most of which belonged to a woman named Helen, a spinster who occupied my unit for thirty-five years before kicking the bucket on a cruise ship. Purchasing Helen's entire estate for a hundred dollars and a case of beer, payable to my alcoholic superintendent, and sifting through the rubble of her life to discover the valuable objects (and discarding the rest of her memories) sparked an unbeatable buzz. I chased that dragon: old people have the best stuff, and if the body is out, then I want in. A walking tour of my apartment is a monument to those who died way too late and couldn't take their teak with them. Every bookshelf, every lamp, every piece has a mental plaque dedicated to its previous owner: Helen the hutch, Carole the lamp, Dinah the chandelier. There is nothing worse than walking into someone's house and complimenting their furniture only to hear that it's named after some IKEA employee and not a dead senior citizen. Not to belittle or be elitist, but personally I prefer an Allen key–free sanctuary. What does it suggest about a person who didn't have to put a stranger in a chokehold to obtain a Danish armchair at an estate sale? (The answer is: lack of adventure.)

For urban treasure hunters, spring is marked with back-to-back church rummage sales, which should not be confused with the summertime casual yard sales for amateurs, or the year-round curated antique markets for homosexuals. A rummage sale is God's way of converting the sacred basements of churches into a Michigan landfill, only to blow the doors wide open to throngs of heathens with fistfuls of cash. The event combines the hysteria of Black Friday shopping with the athleticism of the Running of the Bulls; it is an open expression of at least four out of seven deadly sins. Order is maintained by seniors wearing hand-stitched security sashes, and innocence is upheld by children pushing trays of

Chips Ahoy! cookies and half-filled Styrofoam cups of coffee sold at a four-hundred-percent markup. It is serious business.

Before any rummage sale, I shamelessly convert my church-going neighbors into confidential informants and extract important intel on floorplans and content, so that when I hit the ground, I'm moving with military precision. You walk through the doors and witness the violence of seemingly normal unwashed people hurling themselves into racks of moth-eaten clothes and scrumming around tables of rusted kitchen gadgets and chipped tchotchkes. A rummage sale is the closest thing that I will ever see to a battlefield. Instead of calling it what it is — a toxic pile of urine-soaked bedbug refuse — I quickly generate a story about how some rich, senile lady died in her sleep and her worldly possessions (mainly her stash of jewels) were carelessly boxed and donated to her church by a daft nephew, and that narrative propels me towards the heap in a frenzy. It isn't trash, *it's vintage*, and I will pillage my surroundings like it's a small unsuspecting medieval village, even if the smell lingers in my nose for days.

This compulsive and irrational idea that other people are finding treasure when I'm not is what compels me to swerve across lanes of oncoming traffic at the sight of a yard sale sign. I would offer to clean out a hoarder's house for free, on the condition that when I found a pristine Renoir under a mountain of cat feces and blackened chickpeas, I could keep it. I have genuine panic attacks that by the time I'm able to purchase a fixer-upper, every home will have been swallowed by vacuous home renovation television shows. There are only two reasons to buy an old house: for the unruly spirits that haunt it and the artifacts buried in the walls and floorboards. I would purchase a home with lead pipes, knob-and-tube wiring, paper-thin walls, a crumbling foundation, and no roof sight unseen if a real estate agent even whispered that there might be an old newspaper, a clouded inkwell, a diamond earring, or a mummified rodent to be discovered in its various nooks and crannies. I'd rip the place apart with an axe, complain about the mess, then walk out into the front yard and chop down a glorious walnut tree, plane it down to a single shelf, and display each and every one of my treasures. It would be a private museum for me and my homophobic ghost roommate; while the house lay in ruins, my precious would be carefully protected, stanchioned off with velvet ropes.

There isn't a day when I don't think about treasure. Hunting is a way to assemble a sense of personal history and assign value in a disposable society. There is a difference between price and value: price can be negotiated, but value cannot. Every table of every antique market is run by a storyteller who will haggle not based on the usefulness of an antiquated object, but on an anecdote about how it achieved its patina or wear. In a flea market economy of seemingly worthless trash, nostalgia drives the commodity prices; the weirder the backstory, the greater the value is assigned. A chipped ceramic armadillo piggy bank bought at a thrift store auction for five dollars triples in value when I reveal that I won it in a bidding war with a man who had freshly urinated his pants. Two wooden oxen pulling a chuck wagon become outsider art when I recount how a man nearly punched me in the face because he wanted them but put it down just moments before I picked it up. (Turns out when you snark your FK / LW mantra to a grown man, it triggers his inner pirate and he becomes enraged.) As a result, my apartment is a sanctuary of tiny stories — and I take solace in knowing I could sell everything at a profit and then disappear in a bizarre exploding canoe accident.

SUMMA CUM LAUDE

I'm not just late, I'm hungover and late. As I hustle off the subway, I check my iPhone for text messages. I'm always late; everyone and everything in this city runs chronically behind. I should send my standard apology that reads *Sorry, running late. Subway is a nightmare* but means *I got shit-faced last night, haven't showered, this city doesn't have a comprehensive transit plan, and I was too damn cheap to grab a goddamn taxi, so deal with it.* That just doesn't seem appropriate this particular afternoon.

I amp up to a full jog, hoping my shoes will grip Toronto's unsalted sidewalks. Booze sweat starts to bead on my temples. I don't want to arrive radiating the scent of old beer, so I rip off my toque, unzip my winter coat, and let the crisp February air filter through my sweater. I should have stayed in last night; that would have been a sensible and responsible Friday-night plan. I should have drunk protein shakes or kale smoothies or organic broths while meditating or stretching or cleaning a linen closet — something wholesome, something other than cracking through cans of beer at a house party.

My mouth is dry. Today is all about hydration. My stomach churns with nerves. I should have stopped and grabbed a bite, but I've never been able to perform on a full stomach. *Why am I so nervous?* There is no reason for me to be anxious, this is something I do every day. I'm a pro.

Nearing Rita and Teresa's house, I slow down to catch my breath and zip up my coat. I'm already forty-five minutes late, so another inconsiderate minute won't hurt. Standing on the edge of their property, I assess the curb appeal of the two-story semi-detached west-end home they share. I note the brand new double-pane windows as a sound investment and conclude that these particular lesbian homeowners make conscientious and responsible decisions.

I walk up the green front-porch stairs, but before I knock, I remember the battle plans for Operation Get Teresa Pregnant. My mission: to infiltrate, donate, and leave no egg unfertilized. I fix my disastrous hat head in the reflection of the glass storm door, then firmly knock on the cold pane.

"He's here!" Rita's panicked voice booms from within. "Honey, did you hear me? He's here!"

The wood interior door unlocks and swings open to reveal a grinning and obviously nervous Rita. Her thick, wavy Italian hair, olive skin, and structured cheek bones are toughened by a pair of comfy cargo pants and a crew-neck sweater.

"Heeyy!" she shout-sings, holding the vowel until I pick up on the note.

"Heeeyyy!" I tune back. "The milkman is here!" I kick off the plethora of masturbation jokes and double entendres that will follow.

"Fuck! This is so weird!"

"I know. I'm here to jerk off in your bathroom! Don't tell the neighbors!" I yell for the entire street to hear.

"Come in! It's stupid cold out there!"

As I cross the threshold, we enter a new phase in our friendship. The three of us have known each other for several years, but this is the first time I've ever been inside their home. In a city where people prefer to commune in coffee shops and bars, a first home visit is an open invitation to witness someone's crazy. For the host, it's a yes-I-may-be-a-hoarder-so-deal-with-it-or-leave ultimatum. For the guest, it's a chance to essentially snoop through a physical manifestation of someone's brain. A lot can be said about someone by how they choose to keep house and home.

After a decade of one-night stands, I have developed a quick litmus test that warns when to start looking for the nearest exit. There are four indicators: a dog-eared copy of *The Celestine Prophecy* on an IKEA Billy bookcase, a glass votive candle with the price tag still on, a single cupboard door off its hinges, a twisted and choked-to-death toothpaste tube. If two or more of said items are found, you are more than likely trapped in the home of a murderer. Run.

"Oh my god! Can you believe it? This is crazy." Teresa rushes to greet me. "We're going to do this!"

"I know, right? Sorry I'm late. I went out last night, feeling totally rough." I catch myself sounding like a nineteen-year-old bro.

"Tons of kids are conceived every day to drunk and regretful parents."

Teresa remains unchanged: tall with striking eyes and a dark sense of humor. In 2005, we shared a basement dressing room at Buddies in Bad Times Theatre. She was an accomplished comedian hauled in to boost a festival lineup, and I was the newbie testing out an experimental solo show about grocery shopping called *May Contain Traces of Nuts*. I felt an instant connection to her self-deprecating humor, and our friendship grew slowly over the years. There was no way to predict the circumstances that would lead to us trying to conceive a child together.

"Take off your coat," Teresa instructs. "I can't believe you haven't been here yet."

Since I'm a first-time visitor, I get the customary house tour. A house tour is the standard routine for proud home owners. Rita and Teresa begin to act like real estate agents while I pretend to be an interested first-time buyer. The main floor defines classic Toronto and retains the original layout with beautiful hardwood floors and large moldings. The couple point out key features while introducing each space. "This is the living room. This is the dining room. This is the kitchen," they explain. I play along, nodding and repeating back the words "living room," "dining room," "kitchen" in awe like I live in a one-room mud hut with a family of eight and have never seen a gas range. The entire tour, I scan surfaces for any of the four items on my checklist. *None so far. I'm safe.*

We sit at their mint-green kitchen table drinking coffee and pecking at a plate of cookies. The coffee instantly soothes my head and clears the fog that has impeded my ability to speak in full sentences. Small talk is not my best skill when I know there is a larger task at hand. I want to jump in, do the work, and commiserate after. (Some people need foreplay: I need pillow talk.) We swap recent tales, and for a moment the anxiety of the present situation disappears — we're just friends talking. When Rita and Teresa started to organize coffee dates a year ago, I thought nothing of it. Show folk always promise to meet each other for coffee, because they don't know how to end a conversation. Very few promises for coffee come to fruition. The dates were casually spaced apart so I was unaware of any ulterior motives, but my friends were gradually building up the courage to propose an unexpected arrangement.

Just before Christmas, in the back of a coffee shop in Kensington Market. The caffeine was making me restless, my attention wavered, and I was looking for a polite way out. Then the conversation took a dramatic shift in tone: my friends got quiet and intense and sincere and there was the slightest hesitation in Rita's voice that set off major. warning. bells. I instantly recognized this lead-in. It was more than familiar. My biggest nightmare was fast approaching: my friends were going to ask me to host a fundraiser.

There isn't a shittier gig than hosting a fundraiser. (Coincidentally, there is no better way to become a charity case than being paid in beer tickets, free pizza, and "exposure.")

"Before you go —" Rita's voice quivered. "— we have something to ask you."

"Sure." I prepared to let them down.

"We're . . ." Rita stopped. *What terrible disease could they be asking me to raise money for? It's certainly not a fringe show. It's a burn unit. Burn unit fundraiser.*

Teresa took over. "We're feeling comfortable in our careers

and in our relationship . . . I've always wanted the experience of having a baby and I'm getting of a certain age."

"We . . ." Another false start from Rita.

". . . are looking to start a family. Would you consider being our sperm donor?"

I was gobsmacked. My jaw dropped, my eyes widened, and my face froze, looking like a python in distress. My friends had laid their relationship cards on the table with heartbreaking vulnerability. Milliseconds passed in slow motion as I thought how best to delicately navigate this delicate conversation.

"Oh thank fucking god!" I snarked. "I thought you were going to ask me to host a fundraiser!"

With the big question popped, Rita and Teresa explained their earnest plan. I only half-listened as my mind raced. There would be lawyers and doctors, and we would try to conceive at home using the old-school baster technique. In Canada, a gay man can still be rejected from a clinic even if he is donating to a specific couple; to avoid ballooning costs and disappointment, this was the best way to move forward. They proposed that I would be a "known donor": the child would know that I was its biological father.

The child? Me, a father?

I never considered having children. I never had the aching desire to have a genetic link or to raise a child. It's not easy for gay men to have a baby. No matter how hard we try with one another, it never results in a pregnancy. Unless you have extraordinary financial means, support, or come out of the closet already having a wife and two kids, gay men typically do not father genetic children. *This could be my only chance.*

I am ruled by my gut feelings, which makes me an incredibly

impulsive, unpredictable, highly faulted person. It was a very simple ask: my friends needed something that I have plenty of to spare. Until then, I was like an Amish dairy farmer at the end of a bad day at the market just dumping it down the drain. Hypothetical ifs and buts were abundant, but at the core was clarity and one simple word: "Yes."

Months later, lying between our now-empty coffee cups on the kitchen table is an oversized Ziploc bag filled with large sterile cups. The cups remind us of the real reason for my visit. I'm not here to plan a fundraiser, I'm here to make a baby.

"My doctor donated them towards our little science experiment," Teresa explains. "Hopefully you won't have to use them all."

"I'll be lucky to fill an eighth of one. You can use the rest for storing spices."

With these empty containers with bright orange lids in plain sight, we cannot ignore the truth about this process: in conception, as in comedy, timing is everything. Between lawyers and doctors, Rita and Teresa have planned everything to the nth degree; there is no margin for spontaneity. I have exactly forty-eight hours and two attempts to deliver on my promise, and with such stakes I begin to question if I can physically get a woman pregnant. After a series of blood tests that cleared me to proceed, I still feel deficient somehow, as if I'm not "man" enough.

I have never had sex with a woman. I have a dusty late-'80s, early-'90s understanding of reproduction. As a kid, I used to make paint monsters in art class. I'd take three different colors of bright tempera paint, squish them on to craft paper, fold the paper in half, open it up, let it dry flat, and then add eyes. The results would be these symmetrical psychedelic aliens with googly eyes. If you asked me to craft a representation of the female reproductive system based on education and experience, that's how I would do it. (However, if you asked me to sculpt a penis, I could chisel it from soapstone blindfolded with my teeth.) Now the time has come . . . Teresa's googly eyed monster has released an egg and I must feed it as much semen as possible.

"Let's say we leave you to do whatever it is that you're going to do," Rita says.

"We put a sterile cup in the bathroom upstairs for you. You're all ready to go," Teresa explains.

"Is there a mint too?" I ask.

"Maybe tomorrow," laughs Rita.

Rita and Teresa put on their coats and boots and leave. Once I've finished my one-man sleight of hand, I will text them and leave them to do whatever it is *they're* going to do. I go upstairs and walk down the narrow hallway, navigating a self-guided house tour of the second floor. I dart my head into various rooms, saying, "This is the master bedroom. This is the guest room. This is the office." By process of elimination, I arrive at a closed door and assume that it must be my laboratory.

I push against the shaker door to reveal my biggest nightmare: an unfinished bathroom.

There is simply no bigger boner-killer than an unfinished bathroom. Entering the four-piece room is like entering a 1970s time warp. Nothing about this space inspires an erection: not the yellowed pine wainscoting, not the brown tile, not the hole in the

linoleum where the floorboards peek through, not the leaky fau-
cets. I immediately switch to emergency mode. I sit on the side of
the tub and start mentally renovating the space. I imagine blowing
out the walls, a calming herringbone tile pattern, chrome fixtures,
the rush of emotions that comes from a final reveal. Years of
addictive home renovation reality shows have warped my sensibil-
ities; now my idea of titillation is before and after shots. Aware of
how much time I'm wasting, I push past my sensitivities and get to
the task at hand. I move to the sink, turn on the cold water tap, and
feng shui some necessary Zen into the room.

I unbutton my jeans and slide them down to the floor, kicking
my ankles through the cuffs one leg at a time. I fold the pants in
three equal lengths and place them on the side of the tub. Next, I
dig my thumbs into the elastic band of my gray boxer briefs and
slide them down towards my ankles. *I should have worn a nicer pair
of underwear for this occasion.* I remove the underwear, fold it, and
place it on top of the pants. The act of stripping is performed
unconsciously until I catch a glimpse of myself in the mirror with
my genitals dangling below my shirt. I look like a grandfather
clock draped in jersey knit. I take off my shirt, fold it, and place it
on top of my underwear. Now I'm naked, except for socks.

This is it. "I'm ready to create life," I declare like Dr.
Frankenstein. "Life!"

I reach down and knead my genitals while debating what to
think about during the next one to twenty-five minutes. *Do I keep
it clean, or do I go dirty?* This act is not sex, and it is definitely not
for personal pleasure: I am masturbating with a higher purpose.
I feel incredibly moral. What if at the time of explosion, as millions of sperm jeté from my testicles, these microscopic seekers are

stamped with whatever thought or image triggered the eruption? Should the impetus of life be a new-age affirmation or me skull-fucking my local Starbucks barista? Both options are obscene, but positive thinking is one of the most annoying qualities in a person. Listening to someone muscle through and rationalize a difficult situation with some mantra they gleaned from a cross-stitched wall plaque is not sexy. The only thing hotter than a smiling barista with a French accent is common sense, and I wish I could fold in half and whisper these exact words to my testicles.

Higher education, organic apples, regular paychecks, volunteering, dental benefits. Friction combined with repetitive affirmation means that within minutes I am successfully masturbating using positive reinforcement. I'm a *Psychology Today* article in the making.

My mantra is interrupted by sharp clawing against the bathroom door. Quinoa (Rita and Teresa's antisocial cat) sits outside the bathroom, investigating rumors of a pervert in the house. Like a nosey neighbor, she presses her muzzle into the gap under the door. "Go away, Quinoa!" I beg for privacy as my penis nosedives. Quinoa darts her paw underneath the door like a feline Freddy Krueger trying to kill me in a horrible sex dream. "Scoot, Quinoa, scoot," I plead. Quinoa starts meowing like a siren, her full-lunged territorial cry warning me to drop everything and come out with my hands above my head. I panic and start yanking on my groin like I'm trying to start an old lawn mower. My surroundings take over. *Why didn't they paint out the wainscoting?!* I violently yank and recoil, yank and recoil, over and over. Quinoa mews. "Fuck you, Quinoa! Fuck you!" I shout, stamping my foot towards the door, making my limp Babymaker dance up and down like a dragon head in a Chinese New Year parade.

Until this moment I never believed the philosophical argument that the end justifies the means.

With both hands, I brace myself before letting loose the sexual kraken in my brain. Today's scenario: a Starbucks corporate training video gone bad. Guillaume LeBarista coyly asks me, "Would the ginger man like a ginger cookie?" and the rest is pure XXX Carnal-Macchiato. "I want a cookie! I want a cookie! I want a cookie!" I chant propelling my excitement with each thrust of my own soft hand. Within seconds I can feel that the end is nigh. "This is it," I declare as if it's a sacred pronouncement. "I shall ejaculate."

I look down towards the toilet tank: I forgot to remove the lid from the sterile cup. "Nooooooo!" I silent-scream in horror. "Noooooo!" My aptitude for problem-solving takes over: I instinctively fashion a makeshift ladle with my left hand to catch the imminent eruption. My right hand reaches for the unopened sterile cup. I tear the seal with my teeth and spit the lid across the room. I place the vessel into the sink basin and with my right index finger I spatula the cloudy liquid into the cup without losing a single droplet. I collect the lid from the floor and twist the two parts together securely — the contents safely preserved.

Naked and exhausted, I sit on the toilet, watching the marbled fluid settle and thicken on the bottom of the cup. If this were a one-night stand, there would be congratulatory high-fives followed by a ritual passing of a Kleenex box, but it's not. It's just me and a cup of semen. I think about all the meticulous precautions I've taken as a sexually active gay man to prevent this fluid from harming another person and vice versa. Self-preservation and years of public health warnings have prompted me to perform more spit takes than the Three Stooges. I've always perceived semen as toxic, but in reality it contains half of everything needed to initiate life. Within minutes my seminal fluid will be injected into my friend with the hope of creating a baby, and the fear of hurting someone is strangely absent. My eyes swell with tears: for the first time I see my semen as a beginning and not an end.

I put on my clothes and text Rita and Teresa; on their arrival we exchange goodbyes and I promise to return the next morning for round two. I leave tender and swollen, having learned that masturbating in someone's house without them knowing is a hell of a lot easier than masturbating in someone's house while they are waiting in the frigid cold for you to finish. Riding the subway home, I avoid eye contact with fellow passengers; I feel as though everyone on the cramped car knows how lousy a handjob I just gave myself. I feel the glare of a wizened Portuguese grandmother sex-shaming me, and I carry that judgment as I spend the rest of my Saturday recouping on the couch, watching romantic comedies with a bag of frozen edamame on my crotch.

Sunday starts the same way as the day before: I'm late. This time I run down the street carrying a tube of silicone-based lubricant in my coat pocket and dragging Matt, my boyfriend of five months. Matt is not here of his own volition; I have strong-armed him into meeting the lesbians today, forcing him to confront a new reality in our relationship by making him an accomplice to my bathroom drive-by shootings. Things have been tense between us ever since I diverted our relationship by placing our sex life on hold without offering him a choice in the matter. I flippantly declared my decision without asking his permission.

After the coffee-date-baby-daddy-proposal, I walked north on Spadina and immediately phoned him.

"How was coffee with Teresa?" Matt asked.

"They asked me to be their sperm donor," I blurted.

"What?" Matt shrieked.

"I know, totally crazy. I guess I'm going to be a father. Do you want Indian tonight?"

If my previous relationships were any indication, Matt and I would fizzle and I'd be left single and having missed an important opportunity.

We knock on the door and a similar pattern unfolds: hellos are exchanged, Matt is guided through a house tour, coffees are poured, cannoli are sampled, Quinoa judges, Rita and Teresa put on their coats and boots, I go upstairs to the bathroom, and Matt remains seated at the table.

I enter the bathroom and get right to work. I pop the lid off the sterile cup and obsessively dip my dry finger inside the rim three times. *The lid is open. The lid is open. The lid is open.* This time I'm working with silicone-based lubricant. I squish a generous amount of the slippery solution onto my palms and begin massaging myself. I'm still tender from yesterday's mishap.

It's like I had never done it before. I was all thumbs!

In all my male friendships and relationships, I have never heard a guy admit he is a terrible masturbator. "My hands cramp up and I lose interest" has never been uttered in the history of male self-fondling. Men are idiot savants when it comes to pleasuring themselves. There are no educational games or instructional pamphlets delivered with the onset of puberty; intuitively we know what and how to do it without any formal training.

In grade nine, Mr. Milley told my health class — all boys — that our homework was to go home and masturbate. "Don't be afraid to touch yourself, boys; have fun." Milley's cool approach to sexual education worked for me; I sat behind my desk praying and hoping he'd roll it into a group assignment. I skipped Milley's class only once and inadvertently missed the lesson on the function of the testicles. On the next pop quiz, I answered the question "Why are the testicles situated on the outside of the body cavity?" with "The testicles are needed for balance." When Milley probed what idiot got the question incorrect, I raised my hand. "Whoa, Big Red!" Milley bullied, "I guess you haven't been doing your homework at night."

There is a gentle knock on the door.

"Hey! Are you okay?" Matt whispers.

"Yeah, why?"

"I don't know, you've just been up here for like thirty minutes. I thought maybe . . . is everything okay?"

"No," I snap. "I'll be down in a minute."

"Okay, then," says Matt.

I check my iPhone. Matt is correct: I have been locked in the bathroom for over half an hour. Somewhere between nostalgia and rumination, I lost my grip. I greet the barista, and within minutes I descend from the upstairs bathroom. I text Teresa and the two women swiftly return frozen and carrying a carton of almond milk. With a quick exchange of goodbyes, Matt and I leave. We walk in silence.

"Do you want to talk about it?" I carefully prod.

"No."

"Well . . . thanks for coming . . . It really means a lot. I'm glad you got to meet Rita and Teresa. They're great, no?"

"Totally. Really great."

"No, seriously, let's talk about it. What were you thinking?" I poke.

"Okay, you honestly want to know what I was thinking?" His voice raises. "I'm in a strange house while my boyfriend is upstairs jerking off, apparently starting a family with another couple, and the only thing I want to do is blow out the kitchen and dining room walls and open up the goddamn main floor."

The hurt in his voice warns that I may have caused irreparable damage, that I may have altered our future together. In my attempt to perform a selfless act of friendship, I had become completely selfish in my relationship. On the other hand, Matt's perspective proved that the outlook of most gay men under duress is "open concept." Self-conscious homeowners beware, if a gay man sits sourly in your home, he is more than likely looking for a load-bearing wall.

I'm sitting in a Starbucks at King and Yonge having coffee with a singer who messaged me on Facebook. I've already concluded that she is either going to ask me to host a fundraiser or to father her child. I begin to understand why artists rarely follow up on coffee promises; the conversations are self-indulgent and repetitive.

Teresa's telephone number pops up on my iPhone. It's been two weeks since I left their bathroom looking like a *Law & Order: SVU* crime scene. I slide my finger across the screen and answer.

"Hey, what's up?"

"Shawn. Are you sitting down?" Teresa says. "I'm pregnant! Can you believe it? I'm pregnant!"

Her words reverberate throughout my body. "I got a woman pregnant?" I repeat. I look across the table at the singer and feel instantly radioactive and dangerous. I dramatically excuse myself, fearing I might impregnate her with direct eye contact.

I feel virile and potent and so incredibly high.

In my limited experimentation with drugs, the highest I had ever been was from a hash cookie I ate backstage at Upright Citizens Brigade in New York. I should have taken caution when the cookie smelled like fried chicken, but like a novice I gobbled it down. "I feel nothing," I declared. After an hour-long improvised musical comedy show, I grabbed a hamburger with my friend Monika at a diner. Two bites into the burger, the delicate combo of butter, oatmeal, and hash metabolized with the ground beef, and I felt a tiny door to my forehead open as the back of my skull fell off.

"Mon, I need to go," I stage-whispered across the table in absolute seriousness and for everyone to hear.

"You okay?" Monika replied with a mixture of deep concern and "please don't fuck up my night."

"Yeah, I need to go. I've got maybe thirty seconds before I transcend time and space." I slammed a twenty-dollar bill on the table and started to climb a giant spiral staircase. (Note: the diner housed no spiral staircase.) I had made it four hours into a forty-eight-hour improv festival before being wedged into a yellow cab by Monika.

"Please don't die," she said earnestly before closing the taxi door.

I was subletting an East Village flat adjacent to a Hells Angels clubhouse (which made me feel safer because they always had at least one lookout positioned outside my stoop). I sat in the back of the cab, riding the hash-induced body waves on my way to the flat. Between laughter and trying not to vomit, I annoyingly interrogated my driver: "How much is this going to cost me? Do you think I've been laced? Why is this taking so long? Am I going to die in New York? Where are you taking me?" I was paranoid that I didn't have enough money for what I perceived to be an hour-long cab ride. When the cab pulled in front of the building, the total was four dollars and fifty cents. I had been in the cab for less than five minutes. I paid the driver and fell out of the car onto the street. Having lost control of my legs, I wobbled past the Hells Angel guard, supporting myself on whatever found objects were in my path. Safely inside, I spent the next eight hours transcending time and space.

The next morning, I left my flat in a desperate search for food and coincidentally walked by the same leather-clad guard.

"Hey you!" he yelled.

"Me?" I turned nervously.

"Yeah, you! You were fucked up last night!" He laughed.

A Hells Angel told me I had gone too far in my substance abuse — I felt as if I'd earned a New York badge of honor.

Hearing that I got Teresa pregnant exceeds the high I felt from that hash cookie. I am unprepared for this news, and strangely what I'm experiencing feels nothing like that Creed song. The post-grunge '90s band lied to an entire generation of teenagers with their sweeping saccharine daddy-to-be anthem "With Arms Wide Open." I hear no cymbals crashing or jock vocals as I run up Yonge Street with my arms firmly locked to the sides of my body. I don't want to flail my arms wide open. What if I brush by an ovulating woman and get her pregnant? I'm that potent, that contagious. I am invincible with superhuman capabilities and I desperately need to be quarantined until I can learn how to better control my powers. If not, I could be the semen tsunami that washes over the continents and populates the earth with a baby boom of redheads, my unintentional offspring. I am not ready to lead a sovereign ginger nation.

I stop running. I need to tell somebody right now. I clutch my iPhone and dial Matt.

"I'm going to be a dad."

THERE'S NO U
IN THE WORD ME

I hate sharing.

I do.

I despise it.

I was the kid who measured portions of soda like I was a chemist. It wasn't fair without a weigh scale, funnel, matching glassware, and an eye-level pour. Now I'm the adult who maintains a militarized border down the center of a queen bed, who purchases embroidered "mine and yours" monogrammed towels, who cuts a cake like a cocaine dealer.

In my world, "tapas" means "eat before," and "two spoons, one dessert" is the dumbest suggestion I've ever heard.

By forcing me to share, you are going against what Marie Antoinette died for: a person's right to eat cake while wearing a lice-riddled horse-hair wig. I know my history. I acknowledge that I stand on the headless shoulders of a tooth-rotten aristocracy; still there is nothing more alarming than someone challenging your right to your own dessert. The whole point of dessert is to eat it quickly, emotionally, and without judgment from someone else. I do not need to be distracted from my experience by guesstimating how much of the dessert is legally mine, or keeping a running tally by subtracting how many grams you've put on your fork.

I don't want to concede on the last bite. It's mine.

Even when we order our separate desserts, I neither want to taste yours, nor do I want you to taste mine. I don't need your fork going offside in a hedonist attempt to sample everything. The rules of dessert are simple: you commit to a choice then you live with the consequence of that choice. I'm not advocating for excessiveness; I'm not Oliver Twist with a bowl whining, "Please sir, may I have some more sorbet!"

Everyone gets their own equal portion.

If this makes me a communist? Hello, comrade.

Sharing is stupid unless it's for survival.

If you (yes, you!) and I were trapped on an island together, I'm all for rationing; then we wouldn't be suffering through a vacuous routine of self-imposed restriction.

But, in agreeing to being stranded on an island with me, know I have to be in charge of the food inventory in the supply cave. It is absolutely imperative that when we are forced to share everything, that it is exactly fifty-fifty (well, my fifty plus a small convenience fee paid in a percentage somewhere between three and five percent. So more my fifty-three to your forty-seven).

I also get to drive the bamboo tiki golf cart I built from the wreckage of the crash. You may borrow it when I'm not using it to get to and from work. (One of us has to have a job.) It's physically exhausting being the island's only cartographer, as I spend hours trekking the terrain, claiming this undiscovered paradise in the name of Supreme Leader Shawn. Truth is . . . I'm starting to feel a little burned out, between full-time exploring, my volunteering at the supply hut, and fulfilling your expectations as omnipotent ruler. You could help out a bit more. I'm just saying, it will be nice when you start feeling better and can help around the three-bedroom water-front solar hut (I built for us). Once your fever breaks and you're fully recovered from being gored, which I'm still sorry about.

I didn't know I would react like that. Who knew I would drive the polished shiv I was using as a dessert fork through your hand when you tried to taste my government issued portion of roasted pineapple? First, it is very difficult to get a pineapple to caramelize over an open fire. Second, even though we're the only two people on this island, I still need to feel like I have something that is mine.

Plus it was the last bite.

You know how I get hangry.

Please don't die. You're my only friend.

I AM JONI MITCHELL

Holding a baby comes as naturally to me as holding a nuclear fuel rod. Teresa and Rita coach me from the sidelines on how to support her head and constantly reassure me that my body will not randomly contract and wring her like a sponge. I cradle her against my black hooded sweatshirt. *You dressed in jersey knit to meet your genetic link? I should have come clean-shaven and got a haircut. I'm making a terrible first impression.* There is a veiled tension in the room: we are all vulnerable — even Quinoa, the cat. We collectively understand that what happens next will set us forth on an irreversible course.

There is a thirty-day window after signing an adoption agreement in which you may renege on your decision to waive your paternity; it is a legal undo button that you can press to go back on any agreed-upon terms and conditions and assert your paternal rights. This is the gray area of being a sperm donor or surrogate and the theater of family law, which profits on the unknown.

The great fear is that once you hold your biological child, a caveman response embedded in your DNA will kick in and you'll grunt "me want baby." It is a decision based on instinct and it trumps all reason. This possibility overshadows every altruistic intention and promise because only when you hold the child you helped create is the primitive coin tossed. Heads, everyone breathes; tails, everyone loses.

I can see my face in hers. My eyes are her eyes, my lips are her lips, my nose is her nose, and my cheekbones are her cheekbones. If I were dragged into a police station and given a lineup of week-old newborns and told to point to the fleshy lump that has half my genes, without a doubt I would pick her. That's how clearly I see myself in her: it's like someone took a wool-knit version of me and shrunk it in the dryer.

The love that I feel towards this child is unaffected, and the simplicity of this moment is clean. It defies the cinematic depictions that form my preconceived expectations. There is no room for aggrandizing; it doesn't need to be plumped, exaggerated, or spun.

"She's really beautiful. She is perfect," I say. "I need you to know that she is yours."

Rita begins to cry, and collectively we breathe.

"Shawn, you can't suck and blow at the same time," said my ginger-haired lawyer.

I had spent an entire afternoon searching the internet for a lawyer who practiced reproductive law in Toronto, and when I got over-whelmed by the options (and underwhelmed by the web design), I selected Shirley — she had red hair. But now that I was sitting across her desk cluttered and stacked with case files, I could clearly see from her dark brunette roots that it was a rinse. *At least she's an ally.*

"Puerto Vallarta 2005!" I replied. Shirley looked at me, waiting to understand my joke. "You *can* suck and blow at the same time in Puerto Vallarta! . . . Puerto Vallarta is a gay destination . . . I was there for a month performing . . . making pesos. I have a compul-sive need to please in a resort town . . ."

Half-amused by my crassness, she waited for a joke coroner to enter and pronounce the bit dead before she continued with her rehearsed introduction, which quickly summarized the various points of case law surrounding adoption, donation, and surrogacy in Canada. *That joke cost twenty dollars. Be more serious.*

"Moving forward, you must acknowledge that it is not the right of a father to deny his paternity, it is the right of a child to a father," she stated. "It is this precedent that turns a well-intentioned act into a financial argument down the road, as child support may become an issue. Do you have any questions before we start?"

Shirley picked up a lengthy donor agreement written in coded legalese, sent by one law firm to another to be deciphered and trans-lated by the billable minute. Using the law of common sense, I went through beforehand and wrote "BAD TOUCH" beside any clause that made me feel like a deadbeat dad. She quickly scanned the doc-ument in silence and added yellow sticky notes to problematic para-graphs while I continued down a rabbit hole of overthinking.

I squirmed in the chair, but I wasn't nervous. I had been squirming for the last six months, and as the bump in Teresa's stomach grew, so did mine. WebMD told me that I was experiencing surrogate emotions, phantom responses associated with first-time fatherhood. I cried at bank commercials, ate ferociously, stared at toddlers, and became nauseous at the sight of any baby bump. Stretch marks appeared on my body and on my personality. I was not myself. I did not recognize this person draped in a collection of knits and pleats (inspired by Tom Hanks), the person who made emotional purchases at outlet malls, the person who leered at children, the person who wasn't comfortable in his own body.

The legalese document conflicted with my common sense, and for the first time I found myself questioning the entire process. Even though lesbians and gays have been making babies using the baster technique for decades, the laws surrounding surrogacy and sperm donation are based on Protestant beliefs and archaic definitions of family. The result is a schism: on one side are the clauses and paragraphs that set the rules of engagement for future legal battles, on the other side are emotional commitments and promises. What connects the two is fear.

"Shawn, this comes down to one thing," said Shirley. "What do you want?"

"What do I want?"

"Yes. What do you want?"

Shirley's question was simple, but it felt dangerous. It went against the altruistic ideas on which I donated my size-thirty waist, my sex life, and a baker's dozen of ejaculations all without a single expectation in return. Her question was meant to agitate — and it did. Shirley's only intention was to protect my interest, identify my wishes, and apply them to the rule of law because altruism and liability are unfortunate synonyms in legal matters.

"I don't know."

"Shawn, you have rights as a father and as a donor," she said. "I need you to go home and think hard about what you want and let me know how to move forward."

I left her office, and as I walked up the gradual slope of Yonge Street, my dad costume rattling against a wind tunnel of newly constructed condominiums, I was singularly focused on answering this question, and with each step forward, my anxiety grew and grew and grew. It's not like I hadn't been asked before what I want, but this was the first time I had to firmly assert my wants and needs.

When we started the process two years ago, there was no way of predicting the emotional roller coaster that was before us. Perhaps my irreverent nature was to blame or perhaps the bubble that I live in as a gay man completely shielded me from the intricacies of baby-making, but I didn't know that while trying to create life, one must also weigh the possibility of death.

"We lost the baby." Teresa's voice was somber on the phone.

"Oh." I leaned against the bedroom wall and slid down it.

"Are you okay?" she asked.

"Me? I'm fine. Don't worry about me. I'll be okay. Are you okay?" I spun the conversation.

I was not okay.

Teresa was very matter of fact about the details that led to this loss. We were five months into the pregnancy and we had defied the fertility odds by conceiving on our first attempt. While they were preparing for the baby's arrival, I was removed from the day-to-day reality and spent most of my time marveling at my own virility while smoking an imaginary cigar. My potency had been a crude joke. But now I recognized the profound loss my friends were experiencing;

I felt responsible, but as a donor I didn't know if I had permission to grieve.

A DNA test would ultimately clarify that Teresa and I were a good genetic pairing, with no abnormalities written into our respective sequences. We were perfectly able to conceive, but this particular pregnancy was not meant to be. Though science had proven the existence of bad luck, I believed that I was somehow deficient and that my involvement had directly caused this to happen. The idea weighed on me and permeated my disposition; my brief machismo transformed into a long-standing broodiness.

After a period of healing, we all started the process again, timing my masturbatory habits with Teresa's hormone spikes. Over the next five months, my patience grew thin; masturbating was like brushing my teeth and my iPhone became a black hole for pornography. I would break out in a cold sweat if anyone touched my phone, knowing very well that I was one finger swipe away from being branded a deviant. The effects of pornography quickly diminished and food became foreplay: a box of chocolate chip cookies worked like Viagra. I started gaining weight as, hormone spike after hormone spike, I delivered partially filled sterile cups with the panache of a sad and bloated birthday clown making balloon animals over the bathroom sink.

We would conceive again and the news of this would alleviate some performance stress, but anxiety reintroduced itself as we cautiously moved forward. I was completely removed from the day-to-day milestones of watching the fetus grow and preparing for its arrival. I was, via text messages and emails, nervously following someone baking a nine-month-long soufflé.

The question posed by Shirley was the second triggering question that had been uttered by curious tongues. As doctors gave my lesbians an optimistic thumbs-up on the pregnancy, I had begun sharing my experience with some people close to me, and their immediate reactions were not congratulatory, but invasive. Since I was a walking shitshow, I'd hoped that in sharing the news I'd provide an explanation for not only my temperament but my wardrobe. But the story around childbirth is so scripted that diverging from tradition challenged even the most liberal minds. I wasn't expecting firm handshakes or shots of whisky, but part of me wanted to be indulged in the traditional narrative of expecting fathers, in the heterosexual normalcy — even if it was temporary or pretend.

Instead, I always got a blunt "So, what are you?" in response. Then we'd play out an informal game of Animal, Vegetable, Mineral as they tested the particulars of my situation against their own classification of dads until it generated an insufficient and idiotic portmanteau: gunkle (gay and uncle), dado (dad and donor), pather (paternal and father), proxpa (proxy and papa). I became disappointed that Broadway's paternity whodunit, *Mamma Mia!*, might be the furthest we've pushed the definition of fatherhood. Unfortunately, there were no Grecian islands, chiseled snorkelers in board shorts, or the ABBA songs to make my situation a toe-tapping good time. What I was experiencing couldn't be made accessible with an eleven o'clock number and wedding finale.

The two-year story was culminating in an emotional cliffhanger, and as we neared the finish line, my dad-pants were like two sails pulling me off an edge.

What do I want?

I want it to be fucking over.

I trudged home, ate myself to sleep, and the next day I emailed my ginger-haired lawyer and told her exactly what I wanted: "I want this child to have two amazing loving moms and however I legally fit into this scenario, it is fine by me. I need this to be over."

With all parties in agreement and the process for adoption in place, thoughts turned towards celebration. Three weeks before the expected due date, a shower was hosted for the mothers. The e-vite I received would have seemed impersonal if it hadn't been accompanied by several text messages confirming and reconfirming my attendance.

"Of course, I will be there," I reassured.

It was a beautiful fall Saturday afternoon in Toronto when I let myself into the Queen West home filled with friends and extended family (many of whom I did not know). A process that had been very private and compartmentalized had exploded, revealing a larger community. I was now just a player carrying a greeting card jammed with a hundred dollars in it. *What do you give to the expecting mothers of the child you relegated your responsibility to?* A lame card was only setting up a future of shitty scratch cards and age-inappropriate stuffed animals infused with the scent of old whisky and cigarettes and wrapped in plastic bags.

"You came! Let's get you a beer." Teresa grabbed me by the wrist and pulled me through her home. "We'll get you through this. I'm not going to lie, it's going to be weird."

I walked through the house like the culprit in a murder mystery party. Most were oblivious to my role, except for a few mutual friends (accomplices) and a few suspicious lesbians who worried I was a liability.

"This is Shawn," Teresa said, introducing me to her mother for the first time.

Teresa's mother grabbed me by both hands and reeled me in. "Thank you," she said. "Thank you, Shawn. Thank you. Thank you."

I saw her eyes begin to flood — her heartfelt gratitude caught me off guard. Teresa expertly quashed my reaction by placing a beer in my hand.

"See, I told you it would be weird." She laughed.

What followed was a receiving line to meet the various family members who branch out from Rita and Teresa. At every opportunity, I was made to feel welcome, but I still felt removed, an observer, a witness. Instead of seeing that I was now connected to everyone in the room in a very meaningful way and that I was now a member of a community who would surround a child and support its development, I plunked myself down on an ottoman and sipped a beer. The food table was filled with an amazing spread, and the gift table poured onto the floor; it was a bountiful celebration.

Why not me?

I grinned and beared another hour of casual conversations.

Why not me?

I dismissed the voice until it was screaming in my head.

WHY NOT ME?

I ghosted my own pseudo–baby shower.

I hastily walked home, trying to exhaust the persistent, aggressive voice in my head. The voice that makes me feel selfish and incomplete.

What am I doing? I'm creating a baby with half my DNA and I'm signing away my rights. I will have no say in what this child eats, wears, or learns. I do not get to influence its religious or political beliefs. If some crazy accident happens and this child is put into foster care, I have no legal claim. I've jeopardized my sex life, my relationship, my health. It's occupied every aspect of my life so much that I can't think or talk about anything else and for what? To make other people happy? WHY NOT ME!

Barging into the apartment, I was greeted by Matt, who was sitting in his underwear watching Netflix. Our relationship was so unaligned at the moment that he was a constant reminder of my own selfish pursuit of selflessness.

"How was the baby shower?"

I've always been someone with a high threshold for displaying emotion, but when that facade begins to crack it emits a signal that causes animals within a five-kilometer radius to run for higher ground. I went into the bedroom, slammed the door, and hid under the duvet. I simply could not bear the responsibility any longer. I felt crushed by obligation. It gushed out of me and eviscerated every immediate thought in its wake.

A succession of memories played in my head, and like Russian dolls they fit neatly within each other, memories dating from adulthood back to childhood where I questioned why I felt like a witness but never the direct object of happiness. Christmases, workplaces, bachelor parties, proms, high-school dances, gym classes, sex-ed lessons, romantic comedies, childhood stories, fairy tales, nursery rhymes: I played the role of an alien trying to figure out the customs and rituals and narratives that didn't mirror my own reality.

Oprah Winfrey coined a term for this sort of epiphany: the ah-ha moment. But this is just a euphemism for the oh-for-fucking-fuck-fucking-mother-fucking-fuckity-fuck-sakes moment. This was not about coveting my friends' experience, it was about the sense of removal I felt from a life event that I was integral to but was told I could not have for myself.

"Gay men can't have kids" is a historical, generational, and systemic belief: a dictum upheld by our religious leaders, politicians, lawyers, and teachers; a story told by our great-grandparents, our grandparents, our parents; a lie shared from one gay man to another. I was about to complete the mammalian lifecycle by successfully procreating with a female (and without even touching!), and this directly defied a long-held belief that I was physically incapable of having offspring. I thought I was confronting fatherhood, but in actuality I was probing a deeply rooted shame, an idea that society led me to believe: that I was *less than*. This wasn't about paternity or rights: I did not want to parent a child nor did I crave an SUV stroller and a house cluttered with toys. I was grieving how limited I had been by society because I didn't live within the narrow margins of perceived normalcy.

One would hope this sort of realization comes in a file folder labeled "HERE'S WHAT'S WRONG WITH YOU." A dossier slipped under your doorstep by a jaded ex-lover, a passive-aggressive neighbor, or an anal-retentive sister. It would quickly pinpoint why you like that weird thing in bed, why you play your music too loud, or why you give terrible gifts. Unfortunately it took me more years of consideration to pen that dossier, but in the week leading up to the birth I was offered enough clarity to realize that Teresa and Rita becoming mothers had nothing to do with me, and for the first time in my adult life I was okay with that.

With that gift of my Oprah moment, I went into my second visit with Shirley to sign the formal adoption papers. Teresa had given birth to a healthy baby girl after a long and arduous labor while I had been on a treadmill, happily pacing like a nervous 1950s father. "It's a girl. We are doing well. Thank you" read the text message with an attached photo of Greta.

Her name is Greta.

"Is she a redhead?" asked Shirley.

"She's healthy and beautiful, that's all that matters — but my god I hope yes."

I signed the agreement with a feeling of neutrality. It was a clinical process: a few initials, a few loopy signatures, and the date, October 30, 2012.

"How do you feel?" asked Shirley.

"Well, if I ever get to meet Joni Mitchell at least we'll have something to talk about."

The day after Greta was born, I rented a car and drove up with Matt to tell my parents that they had a biological granddaughter. Matt was a silent partner in this entire experience, and his calm demeanor would help steady the proceedings because there was no way of predicting my parents' reaction — especially my mother's. I never had a confessional experience with either one of them: I didn't have a "coming out" moment that would inform how best to deliver this news. My parents came to realize my sexuality through attrition: I laid it on really thick until they surrendered.

I was coming home to tell my parents that I had impregnated a woman and there was a child with half my DNA existing in the world, so I needed a Trojan Horse. I needed something to get me past the gates and distract everyone until I was in perfect position to drop the bomb. So, twenty minutes out of Egypt, we stopped at a drive-thru Swiss Chalet and picked up a family chicken and ribs dinner (with extra dipping sauce).

"God, this chicken is real good, so fresh. Right, Ian?" Linda said while dunking a piece of white meat in the russet sauce. "What a surprise that you two showed up like this."

"Well, we actually came up to tell you something . . ." My voice shifted into that unstable place that signals you are exactly five seconds away from crying.

Matt clutched my hand to remind me to breathe, and my mother dropped her chicken. "Ah fuck, Shawn! You're dying!"

"No, Mom, I'm not dying."

"You two are getting married! You need money! You got arrested and you need money! You're moving? You need a lawyer? You need money?" My mother rattled off various financial-loss scenarios while I shook my head at her guesses. My parents have always held out hope that one day I might get a tan, but fathering a child was completely removed from the list of possibilities.

"Linda," Matt calmly interjected, "Shawn's not dying, we don't need money, and we're not getting married. Let's just let him speak."

This is the most truthful I've ever been with my parents.

I took a deep breath. "Mom. Dad. A couple of years ago, I was asked to be a sperm donor to a lesbian couple and, well, yesterday a child was born. Congratulations, you have a paternal granddaughter!"

My mother's and father's jaws immediately dropped. Gobsmacked. They froze like cartoon characters and their pupils dilated — you could see the gears turning in their head as they processed the information.

"Jesus Christ!" my father shouted. "I need a drink." He immediately slid out of his chair, abandoned his Swiss Chalet, and ran for the safety of his downstairs bunker. My mother would collect the details; whatever he didn't overhear from downstairs, she would relay once we were gone. I took a photo from my wallet and placed it on the table. Matt and I waited silently for Linda to collect her thoughts.

"Well, Shawn, no need to explain it to me. I get it. Every year your grandfather used to bring a bull into the barnyard to get the heifers pregnant."

The one person I was most afraid to tell summarized what had been a convoluted, complicated journey in plain, old-fashioned farm talk. She didn't ask overly personal questions, she just got it.

I recount my parents' reaction to Rita and Teresa after Greta is safely tucked in a crib in the corner of the kitchen. A reminder that the two new moms are now uniquely connected to an entire clan of weirdos. With the element of fear dissipated, we slowly shift back to our usual ritual of sharing lives through stories — except now with a newborn in the room. We are all raw from this experience, no one more than Teresa, whose body was kneaded and pulled during the birth, but it's a good sign we can still find laughter in our exhaustion.

Holding Greta for the first time, I didn't feel that instant paternal connection everyone feared I would feel. I didn't feel like a father, a dad, gunkle, a dado, a pather, a proxpa. I was filled with a selfless sense of good.

All you can hope for is a child with a fair and equal start at life. *I did good.*

But the unknown still lingers and we recognize its presence as we now move forward, forming our definition of family. I leave our first visit knowing that I get to have a unique relationship that can only be defined by the people involved. I don't have to cross t's or dot any i's, and I don't have to make it neat or tidy or digestible for anyone else to understand.

There is no word in the English language to describe it.

It just is.

DON'T CALL ME MA'AM

"Hi, ma'am!" greets a local Filipino nanny walking in my direction.

Ma'am?

I quickly swivel my body a full three hundred and sixty degrees, hoping to discover a female walking just steps behind me. Years of low self-confidence have taught me that when strangers wave or smile in your direction, it's intended for the more attractive person standing behind you.

Nope.

On this bright sunny morning, there is not a single human of any sex in plain view. The nanny is clearly addressing me. Nanny steps into my path, forcing me to stop on the narrow sidewalk. She uses a tiny newborn baby cradled in a sling to buffer our forced interaction.

"Look, baby," she says while propping the infant's arm to wave. "It's the nice lady we see all the time. Hi, nice lady!"

The fact that this nanny is Filipino bears no weight (I assume they have similar soul-crushing gender roles and pronouns in the Philippines), but my only remaining shred of dignity rested on the slightly bigoted hope that this was a hilarious language mix-up.

This is not a mix-up. I've just been called ma'am. Not madam, but ma'am?

I have a long history of my gender being openly questioned by strangers, but ma'am is devastating. A devastation amplified by the fact that I last shaved a week ago and my face is covered in a patchy coat of red bristles. So either I am a woman of a "certain age" employed by a circus, or I am woman of a "certain age" with an awful jawline rash? Ma'am does not bode well for my confidence, which is already tender considering I feel like I leave the house dressed like a member of a women's curling team every day.

I have absolutely zero qualms with being confused for the opposite sex. I have always embraced the comedy of my androgynous features, and I frequently compare myself to Tilda Swinton or David Bowie (well before Conan O'Brien did). In high school, I had a music teacher named Mr. Geene who thought I was a girl for two years until my voice changed. (I laughed almost as hard as my teacher did when he told me.) Well into my twenties, all it took was wearing a pair of Gap capris into a grocery store to elicit "What is that?" from a precocious, gender-conforming shithead child. When I turned thirty, I threw myself a tasteless bar mitzvah so that I could publicly declare myself a man before my family and community — because there was serious doubt.

I thought that my thinning hair, baritone voice, and general weight gain would eventually settle this confusion, but this is the curse of having a slight jaw, striking blue eyes, and high cheekbones. I'm neither prepared to grow old as a weird-looking gay man, nor deal with the exhausting pressures that come from being mistaken as a homely woman.

My body continues to disgust me on a daily basis. Recently, I plucked what was either a palm of ten tiny hairs sharing the same follicle root or a feather from my forehead. *A motherfucking feather???* Of course, in crisis I turned to the internet, only to see a photo of an infant with a feather protruding from its neck, which is definitely not reassuring. My Google history is a cache of self-hatred as I desperately seek exercises to target "base of the penis fat" only to learn there is no way to directly target penis fat. *What is the evolutionary purpose of a pubic-bone fat deposit?* Various parts of my body that have never before touched have suddenly decided to start rubbing together. A casual walk leaves a trail of denim gratings and my jeans worn thin in the crotch from two thighs that crash like cymbals with each step. My eyelids have become an avalanche of skin, and any respectable plastic surgeon would refer me to a mohel to perform the world's first double-eyelid circumcision. I was speechless when my chiropractor informed me that I had the posture of a sixty-five-year-old. Bad news when delivered by a gorgeous Italian doctor named Vincenzo is terminal. What's worse, I have no idea if I let Dr. Vince crack my central nervous system like bubble wrap because he's qualified or because he's hot, smells of lavender, and sometimes puts his entire thigh across my chest for no discernible reason. *I now pay to have an attractive straight male touch me?* The best future I can hope for is to be a hunchback creature from a Guillermo del Toro film who goes on solo vacations to Thailand.

I need to save for retirement so that I can afford to have sex!

I stare in horror at Nanny's dumbass smile as she waves a limp baby chicken wing at me. In five seconds, every insecurity about my body and age has gushed in silence over a single gendered noun, and it takes everything in my will not to correct this innocent misnomer. I've never found the right tone to assert, "I'm actually a man," without sounding like a complete dismissive asshole.

"Good morning, baby," I coo.

"Bye, ma'am," Nanny calls out. "Have a nice day!"

I leave Nanny and continue down the street towards my local Starbucks. There is a long queue of businessmen who are on their mid-morning trek for caffeine. I snake and shuffle until I am eventually greeted by a bleary-eyed barista. I take a step forward and the barista makes eye contact with me.

"What can I get for you, miss?"

I quickly swivel my body a full three hundred and sixty degrees, hoping to discover a female who has cut in line behind me.

Nope.

"I'm sorry," the barista quickly corrects himself. "I meant, sir. What can I get for you, *sir*."

"That's okay, I'll take miss." I shrug. "I'm comfortable with miss!"

HOLY CATRIMONY

I sit on the edge of the bed, petting Stevie, who is unknowingly enjoying her last few hours in the apartment. She's ensconced on a yellowed and coverless duvet, licking her long thick Maine Coon coat. She has taken well to the brand-new mattress flopped on the floor and sandwiched between two milk crates, interim replacements for the wood side tables that flanked the bed until four days ago.

Stevie hikes her leg like a chorus girl and continues cleaning herself. She appears without a care, even when the various objects and pieces that create her contained world have been sold, repositioned, or have disappeared entirely. Cats, unlike humans, do not let the outlines of missing furniture pieces and the faded discolorations of paint haunt them.

You are no longer mine, I am no longer responsible for you.

Even as a gay man, it is very difficult to have a heart-to-heart moment while someone is nuzzling at their own anus.

No one really owns a cat. You open the door and they become your new unemployed roommate who then pukes on the floor and scoots on the carpet. You leave in the morning and come home eight hours later only to hear them whine that they're hungry — even though they slept all day. They become the zany character in the sitcom of your life, pouncing in and out to break or create tension, depending on the episode.

"You're going to love your new home," I whisper between strokes. "It's going to be great! Change is good."

A huge wad of sadness climbs up my throat, bypasses my nose, and explodes out of my eyes. I fold myself on the bed and between gasps I press my face against her fur, partly in desperation, partly hoping that once — just once — she might reciprocate with a there-there-hello-needy pat on the head. Her tail whips my face in annoyance, then she springs off the bed and saunters out of the room.

Oh, I'm the clingy one?

"Enjoy your eviction, Stevie!" I curse.

In September of 2010, Matt and I sat on the shaded embankment in Riverdale Park, and I nervously pulled at the long, uncut grass. He'd just returned from a summer working in Charlottetown, and his two-month absence had made me grow more curious and eager.

"What would you say to building a life together?" I asked.

It was a blunt and premature question, considering our relationship was only burgeoning, but something told me that a life with this weirdo who dressed in skin-tight purple velour sweaters was worth investigating.

"I think that would be wonderful," Matt replied.

I had no image of what a life committed to just one person looked like, but however it would manifest, it would now include four legs and a tail. Matt and his cat, Stevie, were a package deal, and their story would inevitably become our story.

Growing up, we were always careful never to name the animals: once you gave an animal a name, it became very difficult to eat. (My sister has not eaten pork since she discovered she'd unknowingly eaten Arnold, her beloved childhood pet pig.) There were defined strata of animals: livestock we protected in the barn, hounds and feral cats we sheltered in sheds and haylofts, and pets we kept inside. Rarely did an animal come inside the house alive, with the exception of the two cats that slipped past the screen door and demanded room and board.

My mother hated cats, but not in a cruel way. Occasionally she'd bust out her "in my day we used to drown them in a rain barrel" speech, but that was the unforgiving reality of rural farm life. She felt burdened by the mess they created, and she spent what little downtime she had between working two jobs compulsively vacuuming plumes of shed fur off the furniture. My mother was the type who inspired shame and guilt in visitors reminded of their own subpar cleaning standards.

"Sorry, this place is a pigsty," she would announce before leading guests through her pristine home.

Cats challenged her at every opportunity because there is no reasoning with a poorly behaved feline; a cat does not care about maintaining the factory-like condition of your furniture, curtains, or rugs. A cat concedes to defecating in a box in exchange for food — no more, no less.

Hayley was the cat from hell and my father's best friend. She was a problematic cat from the moment my sister brought her home: a gift from her first boyfriend after his cat gave birth to a litter of satanic beasts. (My sister continues the practice of giving obnoxious white, middle-class names to animals.) In no time, Hayley grew vicious and destructive, and the responsibility for cleaning up after the cat had either urinated on the rug or clawed through the upholstery of an armchair defaulted to my mother. My mother screaming and cursing while scrubbing a fetid stain out of her new broadloom was a primal ritual worthy of documentation by behavioral therapists. The cat hated everyone except my father, and Linda desperately attempted to balance the cat's violent mood swings with vet prescribed sedatives and serotonin reuptake inhibitors. But not even mainlining a tranquilizer would stop Hayley from irrationally hissing, scratching, attacking, shitting, or pissing.

"Every day I put a dollar away, and one day when I get enough money, I'm going to kill your father's fucking cat," my mother confessed over the phone. She also confessed to having a Cool Whip container filled with loonies in her closet.

At any point my mother could have afforded the three hundred dollars to have the cat euthanized by the doctor, but she happily premeditated its demise. One dollar at a time, that's how much my mother wanted her home back and her husband to listen to her.

Six months later, she told my father to say goodbye to Hayley for the last time (he, of course, thought she was joking), and after he left for work, she drove the cat and the Cool Whip container to the veterinarian. She held Hayley, told her that everything would be okay, and wept as the cat took her last breath and drifted asleep.

Later that afternoon, my father found my mother lying in the backyard sobbing in pain; to her left was a shovel and to her right was the dead cat in an old pillowcase. She had attempted to bury the cat but couldn't cut through the clay soil with the blade, and the force had thrown out her shoulder. My father lost his temper and threw all the cat's worldly possessions on to the front lawn: the litter box, scratching post, toys, Christmas stocking, and wicker bed. The only remnant of Hayley's existence would be a small tube of hairball paste that my mother kept as a trophy in the spice cupboard for years to come.

This true crime episode was relayed to me over the phone first by my distraught sister, then by my inconsolable father, and finally by my mother who sat alone at a nearby Tim Hortons.

"I had some money left over from the Cool Whip container so I bought myself a vanilla cappuccino," Linda confessed without any irony.

I was coming out of a meeting when I realized that my phone had been on silent.

Matt called three times.

"Hey, what's up?"

"Stevie is going to die."

"What? Where are you?"

"I'm in a bush." His voice was choked with tears.

Matt had taken Stevie to the vet at my insistence. She had been ill for days and when she stopped drinking water, I bullied him into making an appointment. A three-hundred-dollar exam revealed that she had eaten a thread and it had knotted around her digestive system; it was slowly killing her. He was given two options: either put her down or cough up thousands of dollars for a lifesaving surgery.

Matt was going through a period of extreme unemployment and had scrounged to pay just to get this devastating news; whatever he chose, he would have to borrow money, but he definitely couldn't afford the surgery. The doctor gave him the night to make a decision, and Matt walked home with a turgid cat in a carrier. When the reality that he was about to lose Stevie hit, he burst into uncontrollable tears and hid out of embarrassment.

Matt was sobbing behind a shrub in a stranger's front yard.

The moment I have grown to love most about anyone is when I recognize who they were as a child. Few adults live unguarded, and for very good reason: walls and distance are pillars of survival. Sometimes a glimpse is offered as you watch someone eat a bowl of ice cream or snort too hard at a joke, but witness someone in deep anguish and you will see their inner six-year-old completely unguarded. In this unaffected window of opportunity, you will either introduce yourself or walk away.

Hello Matt. My name is Shawn.

I've heard my father cry three times. First, when Andrea the cat (yes, my sister named her) was hit by a car. Second, when my grandfather Clarence died of melanoma. Third, when Princess

Diana was killed in Paris. They were choking sounds, more like mournful wheezes, emanating from the basement, and you couldn't help but interpret them as a deeply personal invitation to spy.

Princess Diana remains an enigma. *I get it, but I don't get it.*

My grandfather's passing was a turning point in our family. His death was expected, and his rapid decline was shared through anecdotes of morphine-induced hallucinations that caused him to scream, "Don't let that goddamn barn cat into the house! For Chrissakes. Get it out! Get it out!"

Andrea's demise remains a childhood horror.

Cats evolved to mimic the sounds of a human baby, and because of this, there is no forgetting the shrill sounds of an injured or dying cat. My mother was on the phone with Cathy Smockum doing the Sunday night roundup, making sure nobody in Egypt was maimed or missing, when the guttural and piercing vocal siren came from outside.

My father bolted out the back door, yelling over his shoulder, "She's dying! Linda, she's fucking dying!"

Andrea had been clocked by one of the Sunday-night cottagers zooming down Egypt Side Road. The cat had dragged itself from the ditch, across the yard, and onto the deck just trying to get back inside for help. "Gotta go, Cath. I think the cat's dead." My mother hung up the phone and rushed outside.

I remember her immediate assessment. "Oh god! Oh good god!"

She ran back in, grabbed her car keys and an old bath towel, and ordered us, "Do not go onto the back deck, y'hear?"

Lori and I huddled watching TV until they came in an hour later.

"I'm sorry," my mother said. "We tried everything."

Without saying anything, my father went back outside and

washed off the deck with a garden hose, then he grabbed a shovel from the back shed and dug a hole beside the largest pine tree. We were sent right to bed. An hour later, Ian entered, kicked off his boots, marched downstairs, and began to wail. Curious, I tiptoed to the top of the staircase and perched myself there, trying to decipher the sounds.

Who are you?

I heard Matt hurting in a way that compelled me to get closer. I rushed over to his apartment and we sat on his sagging bed, quietly comforting Stevie while devising a plan to keep her alive. Both euthanasia and surgery were too expensive, but if Matt medically surrendered her to a shelter with a no-kill policy, he'd lose custody but she would live. She would live another life but with a new owner.

The next morning, Matt signed a document that declared himself an unfit owner and paid a nominal administration fee. Without a goodbye, Stevie was coldly taken from his possession and prepped for surgery, and Matt returned home defeated. But his capacity to park his own needs for the well-being of an animal made my heart swell.

I love you.

Now, without incriminating myself, it is imperative to gloss over the various details of how Stevie came back into our lives. I, SHAWN HITCHINS, hereby invoke the Carly Simon Act of 1972. (The artistic license in which the singer/songwriter kept the identity of the subject of her hit song "You're So Vain" a secret for decades and everyone was okay with it.) If one needs details: one could imagine a long grift wherein a joint was cased, a decoy dame was used, and everyone involved was wearing a fedora. Or one could imagine me wearing a latex face and rappelling into a clinic from a skylight, *Mission Impossible* style. Or one could imagine a fundraising calendar of topless men holding cats helped us reach our financial goal! The factual and needed information is that I adopted a cat for a man, and I'll leave the question of consequentialism for the *New York Times*'s ethicist.

Both Stevie and Matt would come to live with me, and we would build a life together as promised, the three of us sired together in Holy Catrimony. I had closed myself to the idea of pet ownership after the tragedy of Andrea. In grade nine French class, we had to write a poem *en français* about one of our best friends. But I had no friends, so I wrote a pathetic poem about Hayley. "*Hayley est un chat!*" confessed the last stanza.

I hated that cat: she was the worst best friend I didn't have. I swore never to own a pet after Hayley, but there I was, walking home with a cat in a cardboard box. This story became our annoying couple story, the story we would default to telling at dinner parties, our go-to anecdote for when conversations needed stoking. It was the foundation of our relationship.

Six years later, with our life dismantled, our assets divided or sold, and Matt's possessions in a bachelor apartment at Bathurst and St. Clair, I tell myself this story one last time. I can rationalize the end of our relationship and trace the chain of events that mark our amicable departing. I predicted it, fought against it, and I lost.

But there are no Hollywood feature films or instructional booklets on how to break up with a cat. It's only natural for the cat to go with Matt and for their story to continue together without me, but I'm not prepared for the idea that Stevie may eventually sit on another man's chest and absorb his anxieties; I'm not prepared to like Christmas photos of her on social media; I'm not prepared to hear a new annoying couple story involving her.

Stevie was the witness to our most intimate moments, the subject of our inside jokes, the source of our couple-isms. She was the cause of most of our disagreements. She tested my patience as I channeled my mother, crying after Stevie smeared feces all over the hardwood, or vomited a twelve-inch hairball on my favorite piece of luggage, or nested in my best pair of black dress pants. It would be too cynical to say what remains of six years together is a clawed up armchair and an empty promise to have it reupholstered.

I couldn't picture what a committed relationship looked like, either because I felt undeserving or I was too scared to get hurt. For me, learning to love someone fully and deeply meant allowing myself to love a cat again. It meant knowing one day I might have to experience the irrational sadness that comes from having to say goodbye to a cat.

Matt knocks on the door.

Strange. He has keys but doesn't live here anymore.

He enters and I can feel change in motion. It's a lovely two-hour visit that begins with grilled chicken and asparagus and ends with us trying to coax a larger and older Stevie into a cat carrier.

"I'm sorry," I say, kissing Matt on the lips for the last time.

"I'm sorry too."

"We tried everything."

"We did."

"I think we built a beautiful life together."

"We built a beautiful life together."

"I love you," I choked.

"I love you too," he smiled.

Matt and Stevie leave for the last time. I shut the door behind them and slide the murder chain on.

I take two full steps towards the living room before I am breathless. An iceberg of sadness calves in the pit of my stomach and I begin to release an avalanche of disappointment, anxiety, and stress. It is a force that brings me to my knees. I open my mouth to scream but nothing comes out except the aspirations of two vocal folds rattling to touch. It's been years since I've felt as alive, as aware, as I am in this moment. I can feel the blood in my veins pulsing, my ears throbbing, as my body heaves in and out.

It's just a cat. A motherfucking goddamn cat.

In my most base moment of grief, I allow myself to imagine what I must look like: a grown man piled on the ground sobbing mercilessly over the cat that got away.

I begin to laugh, fully and deeply, while tears stream down my face.

My grandmother referred to sun showers as a monkey's birthday.

My face is wet and grinning: *I am a monkey's birthday.*

I feel six years old.

Hello Shawn.

RIDDLE ME THIS

"How far are you going?" is the first thing out of my mouth when I see an acquaintance on the early morning subway.

It's a power play that forces my groggy-faced friend to instantly confess what station they are getting off at and allows me to determine when the impending unbearable conversation will end. It also gives me an opportunity to execute a Toronto Exit. If I don't want to talk, I can jump off two stops later, pretend to leave the platform by hiding behind a garbage can, then wait thirty-five minutes until the next train arrives.

I do all this to avoid my least favorite question: how are you?

It's such an invasive question, and I feel like I'm being interrogated for the truth. I despise having to gauge and then declare my own emotional state on demand. And, because I refuse to small talk, I just blurt out the truth.

"Well, it's eleven forty-five on a Thursday morning, and I ran out of Nespresso pods, I have to be at a brunch meeting for twelve, I haven't even had my morning massage, and I'm pressing my genitals against this attractive man's hip because he's wearing a nice suit and I'm severely human-touch deficient. And you?"

It doesn't help that I'm severely allergic to anything carbon based, and so the stable-like conditions of a should-be-decommissioned 1970s subway car — ripe with a brew of various perfumes, body sprays, toothpastes, and hair products — make my eyes water and my throat close. So I'm squeaking out a confession, trying to convince you that I'm okay, but there is no way for you to believe it. Every subway ride ends like the Barbra Streisand 1987 camp classic *Nuts*: me screaming, "I'm not nuts!" — but to a jury of TTC riders.

I'm advocating for us to return to simpler times, when riddles and trivia were important life determinants. Your ability to correctly answer a king's knave or impress a blind troll by decoding compounded clues meant that you would keep your head and continue on your hero's journey. Imagine how simple everything would be if all you had to do was answer a skill-testing question instead of answering "How are you?" If all you had to do was remember: first brackets, exponents next, division and multiplication, then finally addition and subtraction. If we could just walk around with Trivial Pursuit decks and every time we felt inclined to ask each other "How are you doing?" we just shouted out obscure questions created in a decade when possessing actual knowledge was impressive.

Moving forward, here's how I wish every conversation on the subway played out:

YOU

Hey Shawn! Been a while!
What did Gail Borden give to the world in 1853?

SHAWN

I don't know! Dental floss?

YOU

(*mimicking a buzzer*) Neeeeaaaagh!
It was condensed milk!

SHAWN

(*genuinely surprised*)
Condensed milk! I would have never guessed that!
(*beat*) Hey, before you go, [INSERT NAME]
(*touches friend's elbow to mimic concern*),
what's the fourteenth highest mountain in the world?

YOU

No. Idea.

SHAWN

It's Shishapangma in Tibet!!
Listen, I gotta go! This is my stop.

YOU

Cool! We should grab a coffee next week!

SHAWN
(*laughs*)
No.

YOU
Perfect!

End of conversation.

A BRIEF HISTORY
OF OVERSHARING

Matt and I booked an appointment with a therapist to talk through our uncoupling — yes, it was a conscious uncoupling in the annoying tradition of Gwyneth Paltrow and Chris Martin. Our therapist, also named Matt (hereinafter known as Therapist-Matt), was a soft spoken artist-writer type who wore black denim jeans and decorated his office with a few Chinese vases, some knick-knacks, and a shoji screen purchased from a local Spadina store.

We sit on a supportive yet firm couch. A coffee table separates us from Therapist-Matt, who sits in a more comfortable looking chair. On top of the table is a box of tissues and a miniature water service that says, "Here, have some complimentary tap water, but not too much." Presumably once you've drank all the water, the intention is that you camel-back your tears by collecting them in the thimble sized tumblers instead of wasting good Kleenex.

Our uncoupling was a year in the making. Matt had lost his job and I had been through two years of hell with a film and television development deal that nearly ended my career. Together we were not only struggling financially, but struggling to connect as a couple. We became threadbare, complacent, a very Netflix and Beef Stew couple. When a tax bill threatened to make me the Wesley Snipes of Canadian theater, I created a one-man yurt out of my duvet. I would sit underneath it for hours, because it kept my shitstorm of reality at bay. Matt would humanely coax me out of my yurt with discounted pans of day-old brownies and squares. (Now, if I went from a ramshackle art-deco apartment to living beside Oprah, if I went from playing small cabarets to stadiums, or if I had a celebrity fragrance that smelled of my two favorite things — the Bulk Barn and white vinegar — or whatever ludicrous comparison we use as a measurement of success . . . I'm pretty sure that I'd still be henny-pennying but under a more expensive organic gluten-free down-filled yurt. I'm not a pessimist, but I am someone who questions the speciousness of something too good to be true. *Okay, I'm a pessimist.*)

When Matt called to tell me that he'd just been fired without any cause or warning, I ran home from the Starbucks I was haunting. I needed to be there when he got home. He walked through the door completely deflated, carrying his favorite workplace owl mug and a company branded exit package. I looked at him and in the flash of a second I saw the next year of our lives play out like a flip book of three-hundred-and-sixty-five stick animations soothsaying the end. This premonition was accompanied by an omnipotent voice that declared: *You will lose everything!*

It was the same booming voice I had heard as I came off-stage at Christmastime, before reading a curt email saying that a multi-platform development deal I had invested everything into was terminated without reason or warning; the same personal greeting I heard after my accountant called me and told me I owed fourteen-thousand dollars to the tax man. They were clear and pointed doomsday declarations. As much as I tried to ignore them, they woke me up in the middle of the night, ordering me to pay attention as I gasped for air.

You will lose everything . . . including your Scandinavian furniture.

Face-to-face with Matt, I acknowledged the voice. It was Thor. (When I start hearing the voice of an omnipotent force, as an atheist, I get to select a ginger pagan option.)

"Why are you crying?" Matt asked. "I'm the one who just got fired!" He was clearly annoyed that I had once again co-opted his own crisis as my own.

"A year from now, we'll be standing in this exact spot but on very different terms," I voiced like a fraud oracle squatting over a Grecian fissure.

"Hmm . . ." Matt was wary.

Exactly one year later my Matt prophesy came true.

Matt now acknowledges that my witch is one hundred percent correct, ninety nine percent of the time. (We started calling it my "witch" after I accurately predicted Joan Rivers's death within twenty-four hours. *What was I supposed to do? Tweet her?*

@JOAN_RIVERS YOU'RE GOING TO DIE. #FYI #GRIMTWEETER #NOTATROLL #RIP

No.) Call it heightened intuition or hyper-vigilance derived from my childhood, my witch is the power to instantly assess any person or situation in front of me with a ten-second speed read and accurately predict the immediate outcome. It is a valued gift, but also a quality I wish I could ignore without consequence.

Matt and I would have a final goodbye exchange in the foyer of our apartment. The various events that conspired to bring about our end were the unpredictable trip stones that served as a humble reminder to surrender to Thor. Cruel and surprising, there was no way to foresee our local independent grocer fold under skyrocketing rents and transform into a giant Dollarama. A loss that interrupted my opportunity to flirt with deli counter ladies for discounted prepared salads and organic meats.

But this is what Thor hath declared: *You will lose everything . . . including your ability to farm-to-table.*

In one of our more intense sessions, Therapist-Matt asked me a real CBC Radio question — a simple yet leading statement, acting as a prompt to disclose any previous traumas capped with an over-sincere "and what was that like?" It is the type of precious interview question where journalism and psychoanalysis cross, which sets my teeth on edge. So, I answered Therapist-Matt with my concise pathology, beginning with a short story of origin, followed by examples of familial strain, and then expanded on the spiraling effects of instability, capped with a few anecdotes of the never-ending, exhausting, draining work of being a Canadian performer, and delivered with a tearful "shit-eating grin" (to quote my mother).

"Shawn, have you ever thought about taking a vacation?" Therapist-Matt yoga-spoke.

"You mean one where I don't have to flyer for an eight o'clock show?" I asked.

"Yes. A real vacation."

Both Matt and I started laughing at this ridiculous word "vacation." And we leaned into the joke as if the essence of the word "vacation" could not be translated into our mother tongues. We started repeating the word like we were the pink and blue martians from *Sesame Street*.

"Vay-cay-shun. Vay-cay-shun. Yip-yip-yip-yip . . . Uh-huh. Uh-huh."

I had been hoping for a clinical diagnosis, a word to name the overwhelming sense of disappointment and obligation I felt. Instead, I was an adult being prescribed a little time off. Shortly after turning thirty, my life flipped from a cavalier extended adolescence to an immediate adulthood. In less than three years, I became a biological father to a child, I mourned the deep loss of a father figure, my career grew exponentially, and I was in a committed partnership. But sustaining these ties grew more and more challenging, and I began a day-to-day existence supported by chiropractors, lawyers, dermatologists, doctors, surgeons, accountants, agents, and now a therapist.

"We probably should have gotten you help years ago," my mother speculates every other phone call. It's the type of afterthought that allows her to *Que Sera Sera* around a difficult subject, to speak in the safety of the now without assigning fault. "Just make an appointment to get your thyroid checked," she urges. "You know goiters run in the family."

Maybe I should have seen a therapist when I was younger. Maybe when I dismantled the family piano, dragged it piece by piece to the garden, then lit a match to it because I labelled the heirloom instrument "gay." Maybe I should have spoken with a professional and learned to take vacations. Then maybe I would have been spared a slew of humiliating blackouts, one night stands, bad jobs, terrible auditions, and destructive relationships.

"Where's the fun in that, Thor!" I stand naked in an open field with my Hugh Jackman ass facing the camera. Forks of lightning crack across the sky and a torrent of wind circles above. "Where's the story in that, Thor?" I laugh as my crossfit body is pelted with rain and hail. "Smote down on me with all your ginger force!"

The therapy sessions turned from an exploration of uncoupling into a dissection of my career as we collectively dug layer by layer to discover why and how I do the things I do — trying to unearth a reason that goes beyond collecting a good story. Years ago, Golden Globe–winner Amanda McBroom — you guys, she wrote the song "The Rose" — told me in the Hogwarts-esque Yale cafeteria that I was stricken with a "divine dissatisfaction." Usually, I'd fluff it off as some new-age-mumbo-jumbo but this person had a Golden Globe and therefore I listened. (If she had won the Oscar, I would have taken dictation.)

"Only someone with a divine dissatisfaction can recognize another, and I'm sorry m'darling . . . you got it," said the chanteuse and songwriter. I committed her comment to memory but probably should have Googled it sooner: its provenance is Martha Graham, who coined it as a way of describing her creative unrest. But its true meaning hadn't resonated with me until I witnessed a fiercely head-strong independence blossom in Greta, now a toddler. Her spiritedness is a direct reflection of our shared essence, which goes beyond bone structure and pallor. "How many pianos will this child set on fire?" is a question that fills me with joy, but along with that comes a lingering sadness knowing that I may not be the one there to hold the fire extinguisher.

My relationship with my father was no match for this force of divine dissatisfaction, but in the one aspect in which we were able to connect — comedy — I've built my livelihood. I am the sum of my father's father's greatest fears. I have learned that what I lived with was a fraction of the brutality my father experienced at the hands of his father. Although this knowledge doesn't excuse Ian's behavior, it does allow for compassion. It allows me to see my father as a child with a generous sense of humor who played the flute in a marching band and loved to draw and knit until his father decimated his natural ways of expression — which has nothing to do with sexuality. The greatest gift my father gave me was his failure to make me invisible.

"What, Matt doesn't like us anymore?" My father reacted to the news of my breakup with a surprisingly personal question. He was diverting from a two-decade-long script which has made me feel more like the syphilitic character in an Ibsen play than a member of my own family. It signaled a shift towards reconciliation. He now attempts to bond by asking, "Do you have a driver's license?" or "Where do you live in the city?" or "Do you like being on stage?" Questions that try to connect with the teenage me who left and not the adult me who's clocking the length of my visits using the timer app on my iPhone.

I have spent two decades negotiating with my early days, trudging through an urban existence carrying my pastoral upbringing on my back, rarely crossing a bridge without an emergency flask filled with kerosene. As I understand my adolescence as an inciting force, that perspective allows me to connect various events with hindsight. It is my nature to test the breaking points of ideas and relationships and to interpret some meaning from the mosaic of those shards. I am ostensibly experiencing a second puberty, a painful and awkward phase of jarring tectonic shifts and rapid change — knowing there will be long reaching effects but my witch is not (yet) able to predict how they will play out. It's the promise of the next adventure. I no longer believe the platitude "things happen for a reason," and I do not believe we are waiting for a predetermined moment to mature. Whatever drives us is behind us kicking us in the ass, tripping us when we're not paying attention. Nothing is ahead of us but what we create from our given circumstances.

I have a daughter with a lesbian couple. I share custody of a cat with my best friend who is no longer my lover. I have a difficult relationship with my father, but I have a relationship. I have a hilarious mother who struggles with change even as her body forces her to adapt. I have a sister who I text every now and then (our relationship has yet to be discovered). I have dinner every Sunday night with a family that is not my own but is my own. I choose to make money by standing on stage in front of strangers and oversharing my brief history. These are my given circumstances.

The linchpin is pulled.

I watch the pieces fall.

You will lose everything . . . including your red hair.

Praise Be to Thor.

I HEAR CATHERINE ZETA-JONES IS AVAILABLE

Shawn Hitchins . . . played by **Tilda Swinton**

> *Tilda could easily pull another* Orlando *here.*
> *The resemblance is uncanny, and there is no other*
> *actor I'd trust to play me. Swinton is a true artist*
> *and spends many years developing projects before*
> *shooting. It would be an intense period of research*
> *that would involve me having to join Swinton and her*
> *painter lover in her Nairn estate for at least three to*
> *ten years.*

Ian Hitchins . . . played by **Tom Selleck**

> *My father has a mustache, and Tom Selleck has /*
> *had, or at least has the ability to (I haven't talked to*
> *him in a while) grow a mustache.*

Linda Hitchins . . . played by **Shelley Long**

> *There isn't a day or an hour or a minute that goes by that I don't pray to the Hollywood elite for a Shelley Long comeback. I have no idea what happened there. Is it because she left Cheers to pursue her film career? Is she the original David Caruso? Or did she just get to the point where she had banked enough cash to walk away? Sometimes I feel like it is my purpose to somehow instrument her return as a leading lady. I bet Shelley Long has a hobby like pottery or an entire library of children's literature that she will publish posthumously (but she will never die).*

Lori Hitchins . . . played by **Neve Campbell**

> *My sister had gravity-defying waterfall bangs that sort of cascaded over her forehead for most of the '80s and '90s. Also, she had a lovely black Labrador dog named Bailey and she would constantly call her name: "Bailey! Bailey!!!" And for these two reasons, I think: Neve Campbell, Party of Five. Plus, Neve Campbell is some serious Canadian content representation.*

Aunt Debbie . . . played by **Meryl Streep**

> *I feel like Meryl is bored with what's being offered to her these days. My aunt Debbie is a great character, plus the prop cigarette will really help Meryl with some needed grounding in her performance. (I'm not*

afraid to say, "Reel it in Streep, it's a bit over the top!") I think there is potential for a Shelley Long and Meryl Streep road-trip movie spin-off?! Plus, if we want to go in a sci-fi direction, then we can tap into a clone storyline by engaging Streep's daughters Mamie and Grace.

Teresa . . . played by **Jennifer Garner**

Jennifer Garner is completely and utterly wrong to play the mother of my daughter, but we need her to secure foreign investors and distribution.

Rita . . . played by **Ellen Page**

Originally, I asked Maggie Q, but she respectfully declined my request by blocking me on Twitter. Page is great, the millennials love her, and with her attached we can get a tax incentive to shoot in Timmins, Ontario.

Greta . . . played by **The Hologram of Judy Garland**

Why are we not employing holograms while entertainers are still alive? Why do we keep dragging exhausted performers onstage to fulfill our hero worship? Instead, we wait for then to drown in a hotel bathtub before conjuring a digital ghost to haunt the stage. If I'm strung out on amphetamines and begging a Danish audience for schnapps, send out my hologram. If I have a needle in my arm while searching for my prosthetic nose, send out my hologram. Maybe I'll survive, go through a period of recovery, and come back with a spoken-word album about my time spent germinating heirloom seeds, but until then: enjoy my verified hologram. Based on the fact that we have the technology to digitally sandwich a dead celebrity face on to a newborn baby, I think Judy Garland would be an amazing addition to the cast. And I would love to see the moment where Tilda Swinton looks down at a swaddled Judy Garland and rejects her. It would be so meta.

George Bloomfield . . . played by **Dustin Hoffman**

Hoffman is my choice over De Niro, and he always has been my preference. Even though George had a great De Niro story, Hoffman is a more generous personality and would probably shave his head for the role.

Ginger Lawyer . . . played by **Sandra Bernhard**

I've met Sandra Bernhard three times, and I've choked at every single opportunity. At this point, I believe the only way I'll have a meaningful connection is to create work for her. I don't have a sardonic lesbian in my life, but I'm willing to verge into scripted reality where Sandra is my roommate and we sit around talking about various hammam spas, complaining about what Marianne Faithfull did or said, and sharing thoughts about mid-'90s fashion designers.

Matthew . . . played by **Ryan Gosling**

> *I think this casting is self-explanatory. We can bend the truth and say the character of Matthew was an exhibitionist.*

P-Town Margie . . . played by **Amy Sedaris**

> *Amy Sedaris is a comedic genius. She would be able to snap between realities of someone who was tortured by extraterrestrials but needs to sell tickets to a seven p.m. show. Think Jodie Foster in* Contact *meets Jerri Blank.*

Stevie the cat . . . played by **Catherine Zeta-Jones**

> *There are several different ways to approach this: live action with cartoon voiced by CZ-J (*Who Framed Roger Rabbit *style); live action using a real Maine Coon cat with a hilarious, snarky improvised commentary voiced by CZ-J (*Look Who's Talking *style); motion capture with CZ-J dressed in a blue unitard (*Lord of the Rings *style). My preference is for motion capture — if only for the selfie of me and CZ-J dressed in unitards, and for the outtakes when CZ-J does an impromptu number from* Chicago.

Quinoa the cat . . . played by **Roseanne Barr**

> *See above comments about Catherine Zeta-Jones and apply to Roseanne — even the* Chicago *number applies.*

I THOUGHT I SHOULD MAKE A SPEECH . . .

This book is one hundred percent because of CRISSY CALHOUN, who not only said "yes" but also said "keep writing" as I encountered life crisis after life crisis (which spurred only more crises that grew like Tribbles). I cannot thank her enough for her editorial eye, laughter, comprehension of the English language, and friendship (in person and through memes, gifs, and *Friday Night Lights* references) over the past three years.

This work exists because of the dedicated people at ECW PRESS who tackle the challenge of developing and exploring new voices when so very few do. *I take off my imaginary top hat and bow towards the team.*

My heartfelt thanks to JEN SQUIRES for your continued ability to shoot around my face, CHRISTOPHER ROULEAU for your font-tastic skills, NATHANIEL BACON for always having my back, and BEN STEAMROLLER for illustrating me with such magnificent thighs.

Dear RICK MERCER, I owe you a bottle of champagne.

Hey MICHAEL URIE, can I borrow a bottle of champagne?

With love to . . . my chosen family (MATTHEW & STEVIE; TERESA, RITA, & GRETA; LOUISA & DACCIA) and my given family (MOM, DAD, LORI, AUNT DEB, & GRANDMA).

My deepest appreciation to . . . JONATHAN SOJA for literally picking me off the ground, PATRICIA TUFF for completing the mission, JENN FRANCHUK for answering my panicked Facebook message, and the BOYS for tagging me in cottage photos while I was on lockdown all summer.

Hallelujah to . . . TANIA WALDOCK & BEAU OPPERMAN for giving a broke writer a steady income and a place to call home when he needed it the most. (I highly recommend the Steak & Wild Mushroom Pie at HOUSE ON PARLIAMENT.)

In honour of the FARMERS OF EGYPT.

In solidarity with the GINGERS OF SCOTLAND.

In memory of GEORGE BLOOMFIELD, CLARENCE SMOCKUM, & ALBERT HITCHINS.

To the friends, acquaintances, drag queens, relatives, & nemeses (or any combination of those five) whose narratives have entangled with mine, thank ~~me~~ you!